D1613301

GOING NATIVE IN MURCIA

SECOND EDITION

A BRIT'S SCRAPBOOK

GOING NATIVE IN MURCIA

SECOND EDITION

DEBBIE JENKINS
MARCUS JENKINS

NativeSpain.com

First Edition Published In Great Britain 2005
by www.BookShaker.com

Second Edition

Typeset in Garamond

Praise for Going Native In Murcia

The book is literally packed from cover to cover with the most incredibly well researched and pertinent, up to date and relevant information that anyone – and I mean anyone – interested in buying property in Murcia, living in the region or just travelling around Murcia will ever require.

If you're about to become a new expatriate and move to Spain and in particular Murcia, this book can act as your guide, you won't want to go anywhere without it! In fact, the information contained therein will become your life map! There is information on every single conceivable topic – nightlife, the property buying process, shopping, the population and map reference of towns, airlines and hire cars, vocabulary, fiestas, money, making concrete! Every scrap of information that Debbie and Marcus Jenkins have gleaned over the past four years is in this book! I love it! It makes fantastic, interesting and even entertaining reading for anyone with even just a modicum of interest in Spain!

Rhiannon Williamson – www.shelteroffshore.com

I just wish I had got this book two years ago, when I was buying my house in Murcia! The Spanish house buying process can be a bit daunting for the average Brit... but the flow charts really make the steps and the roles of the associated people... absolutely clear!

As the book is full of very relevant web–site addresses, the content is actually much larger than presented... and will remain fresher... longer!

Expat... would be expat... or just visiting Murcia for a holiday... this book is essential reading... don't go without it!

John Mellor (Cheshire/Estrella de Mar)

We are coming back out to Murcia in April and have found your book to be an excellent starting point for the areas and things we need to be looking at. Both my wife and I both found the book very valuable in getting to know Murcia a little better.

John Wilson

We purchased your book via Amazon before Xmas and have found it a most useful guide to the area. We are about to start a property search in preparation for a permanent move with family to Spain at the end of the year. Had enough of cold, damp, dreary days (and nights) in Redditch, and the general social decline and rising costs in Britain. So the "Buying in Murcia" flowchart and viewing checklist are going to be most useful, as are the town/village guides.

Congratulations again on a brilliant, practical book.

Rosemary Clarke

Thanks to your book I have already started the ball rolling towards our move to Murcia and have had a meeting with an agents representative who happens to be here in Cowes to spend the holiday with relations.

Ken Meynell

Purchased Going Native in Murcia, prior to our first visit to that region in September of this year. The book is well researched and covers a whole range of information and many excellent website addresses. A must for anybody considering visiting or purchasing in the Murcia region.

Paul McGloin

Acknowledgements

We'd like to thank Joe Gregory our editor and designer, from *www.bookshaker.com*, for his hard work in such a short space of time.

Our thanks go also to Jo Parfitt (*www.summertimepublishing.com*) for her wonderful preface and Joanna Styles (*www.joannastyles.com*) for writing the foreword.

We would also like to acknowledge all of the other adventurers who have visited the area, fallen in love with it and begun the process of making Murcia their home. These wonderful people have provided us with feedback, suggestions, ideas, corrections (there were many for the first edition!) and further inspiration.

In no particular order – we would like to thank our contributors: Mike Penning for providing us with a detailed breakdown of areas for improvement; Mike Birley for providing an excellent and thorough update on the Los Alcázares area; Margaret Poole for her tip on the restaurant in Los Nietos and John Mellor for his excellent list of website links.

And finally, thanks to our families, without their support we wouldn't be here. You're all welcome at the caves, any time!

Marcus and Debs
The Caves, May 2006

Contents

PART 2: BUYING

RESOURCES

Foreword

Most people have heard of Murcia, one of Spain's undiscovered corners, but few know much about it: ask a Spaniard what they know about Murcia and they'll probably mention La Manga and agriculture before they dry up. Put the same question to a foreigner and they're likely to get as far as the Mar Menor, golf and cheap property. But this is just a tiny fraction of what Murcia really has to offer and as this books shows, there's a hidden land out there waiting to be discovered and enjoyed.

Debbie and Marcus Jenkins open the window onto a world of fascinating contrasts: verdant mountain tops and desert rock formations; bustling Murcia city (one of Spain's up and coming must–see destinations) and fabulous sandy beaches that you could well have to yourself; busy expat enclaves and tiny Spanish hamlets. This is a land of Barbary sheep and Montpellier vipers, delicious Zarangollo and Carrascalejo, the Spanish Teleclub and expat bridge clubs. Surprised by the Jenkins' Murcia? I certainly was.

When you arrive somewhere new, you need all the help and information you can get. If that information is first–hand, accurate and bang up to date, so much the better. 'Going Native in Murcia' in its second edition is all of these. This gem of a guide contains vital facts, useful suggestions, handy flowcharts, top tips and helpful websites as well as plenty of valuable advice from the Jenkins who really have been there and done it (and often the hard way!).

If you're planning to move to Murcia, buy a holiday home there or just fancy going to have a look round, allow Debbie and Marcus to be your guides. They're passionate about life in Murcia and their enthusiasm is certainly catching – See you there!

Joanna Styles
Freelance writer and author specialising
in Spain and relocation generally.
www.joannastyles.com

Preface

I may have travelled to or lived in a few countries in my time, but oddly, for a Brit, I hardly know Spain at all. Three times to the Costa Brava has been my lot. Nevertheless the appeal of upping sticks and moving to the land of paella has not escaped me.

When Debbie and Marcus Jenkins decided to move to Spain their friends and family thought it was a perfectly sane idea. But when they heard that the couple were buying not one but three caves in a part of the country that no–one had heard of, and was not by the sea, they shook their heads in disbelief.

A couple of years on Marcus props up the tiny local bar in La Murta like a local and the neighbours have become such friends that they leave offerings of olives and local honey on their doorstep. Debbie and Marcus have so come to love the area called Murcia that their enthusiasm seems to have affected the rest of the world and a new airport is being built to handle the newfound popularity. Maybe they struck lucky, or maybe they have an eye for a trend? Whichever, this cave–dwelling couple do not want to keep their knowledge a secret any longer and now share their hard–won information with you.

Whether you want to go to visit the area and simply explore, or whether you are serious about buying there, this book has it all. From teaching you how to make concrete to suggesting where to stay, where to eat and how to rent a car, you will find your answers here.

I have lived in five different countries myself, and each time have found the first few months of getting to know the rules to be an exhausting task. Debbie and Marcus show you how to act local and think local and how to start the processes of settling in and belonging fast. And the sooner you find that house and find your feet the sooner you can get down to finding the best paella in town.

Jo Parfitt, International Journalist and author of
Expat Entrepreneur: How To Create and Maintain
Your Own Portable Career Anywhere In The World
www.summertimepublishing.com

About This Book

This book has taken 5 years to research and has been a real pleasure, taking us around the whole region that we now like to call our home. The first edition came out in May 2005, when we had to force ourselves to stop adding information and get the book out there! This second edition includes most of the stuff we couldn't fit into the first one plus almost a year's worth of extra experience and knowledge as well as the invaluable contributions from readers.

The book was borne out of the frustration of none of the major guides covering the region, or at best only dedicating 4 or 5 pages to it. When they did mention Murcia they focused entirely on the golf complexes and housing estates. In fact, the only guides we could find that covered the Murcia region in any detail were in Spanish, interspersing flowery language with inaccurate information. So we felt it was time for someone to put this major region firmly on the map.

Murcia is a beauty, with warm and welcoming people, a strong property market, wonderful food and fantastic weather.

Our goal for you as you read this book is that you'll be able to enjoy visiting this region in all its glory – with us as your equally wide–eyed guides. If you're thinking of investing here or even making this region your new home then the sections on buying and visiting will tell you all you need to know.

We, the authors, try to make the information available as accurate as possible, we accept no responsibility for any loss, injury or inconvenience sustained by anyone using this book.

Although inclusion in a guidebook usually implies a recommendation, we cannot list every good place. And we apologise in advance if we missed you out – get in touch and let us know (*www.nativespain.com*). In addition, exclusion does not imply criticism. In fact there are a lot of reasons why we might exclude a place, for example it might not be appropriate to encourage an influx of visitors!

Updates, Changes and Your Feedback

Stuff happens – prices go up, restaurants end up under concrete (no really they do!), places change hands, bad things get better and great things go bad! So if you find things have changed, please let us know. Join our community and pop us an email via *www.nativespain.com*.

Perhaps you have a story to share for the Native's Section? Or maybe you've visited a museum, gone scuba diving or had a wonderful meal. Get in touch, let us know.

Everyone who contributes at *www.nativespain.com* will find their name listed in the next edition as well as "author discounts" on future guides.

We plan to update this guidebook as frequently as possible, to ensure you get the best and most accurate information, probably every two years as our budget permits. Publishing a book like this can be quite costly, which is why for this edition we have allowed a select few advertisers to help us cover the costs. We'll see how this works out; let us know your thoughts too.

Contact us: *www.nativespain.com*

Part 1: Visiting

You'd be forgiven for thinking that Murcia contains nothing more than the Mar Menor, La Manga golf club and a swathe of new–build housing estates catering solely for Brits and Germans. This is the view portrayed by most guide books and many journalists. Yet it's a view far from reality.

It's true that Murcia does have many golf clubs and an increasing population of northern European immigrants and with 320 days of sunshine per year you can see why. But, we also have mountains, wildlife, a city that retains a unique Spanish culture, unspoilt beaches, national parks, snow (though not much!) and wild boar.

Overview

Murcia, covering 11,000 square kilometres making up 45 municipalities is home to just over 1 million inhabitants. It has an airport, which although called Murcia airport is actually 50 kilometres (30 miles) from the city in the coastal town of San Javier. Due to the present location of Murcia airport the city is hardly a well–visited tourist attraction. However, spend a few days there and you won't regret it; it's a great example of Spain and all its character.

Murcia is located on the Mediterranean Sea and forms a small sea of its own, known as the Mar Menor. Some of the beaches of the Mar Menor include: San Javier, Santiago de la Ribera, Los Alcázares, and La Manga.

If you're looking for more than a swim and prefer hiking, we recommend the Natural Park of Calblanque and the beautiful coves and coastal parts that surround this area. For the nature lover, there are a number of activities in the mountains of the Sierra Espuña.

The Climate

You can enjoy the coast practically year–round in Murcia, from the Easter holidays and well into autumn. There are a great variety of water activities, from sailing to windsurfing to water–skiing, scuba diving and kayaking. The average temperature during the year ranges from 11°C in winter to 25°C in summer. The climate is dry, hot in summer and mild in winter. Murcia receives the most sunshine per year in Spain.

The region of Murcia has the typical Mediterranean semi–arid subtropical climate: namely an average annual temperature of 18°C, with hot summers (registering peak temperatures of 40°C) and mild winters (though you still might see some snow higher up) with an average temperature of 11°C in the winter months of December and January.

There are between 120–150 days per year with clear skies and 2,800 hours of sun. Rain is scarce throughout the region (approx. 300–350 mm/year), falling mainly in the spring (April) and autumn (October), leaving the summer wonderfully dry. However, due to geography, the temperature differences between the coast and the interior are much more extreme in the winter. On the coast temperatures tend never to fall below 10°C, while inland at higher altitudes (in the Sierra Espuña for example) they may not exceed 6°C. Areas at higher altitude also show a higher average annual rainfall, which reaches 600 mm/yr.

MURCIA WEATHER							
	Monthly Temp. (°C)	Max. Daily Temp. (°C)	Monthly Rainfall (mm)	Days With Rain (1mm)	Days With Thunder–storms	Cloudy Days	Hours of Sunshine
JAN	10	16	25	3	0	3	170
FEB	12	18	28	3	0	2	180
MAR	13	20	30	3	0	2	210
APR	16	23	27	4	1	1	240
MAY	19	26	32	4	2	1	280
JUN	23	30	20	2	2	1	310
JUL	26	33	5	1	1	0	340
AUG	27	34	10	1	1	0	300
SEP	24	30	27	2	2	1	240
OCT	19	25	44	4	1	1	200
NOV	14	20	32	4	0	2	170
DEC	11	17	21	4	0	3	160
YEAR	18	24	301	35	11	17	2800

Snow and Chumbos – a rare sight indeed!

Food & Drink

The Spanish, like many Latin cultures, make the mid–day meal their biggest, stretching it out for hours. From midday to mid–afternoon, everything shuts down, except of course for the restaurants. Then, after this long, leisurely meal (and sometimes a nap) they return to their workplaces and continue into the night.

The evening meal is late, anywhere from about 9pm to midnight. While most of us are not accustomed to eating dinner so late, you might consider indulging in the Spanish favourite, tapas, as a light supper, although no real Spaniard would ever do this.

Restaurant hours are typically 1:00pm – 4:30pm for lunch and 9:00pm to 12:00 midnight for dinner. Though this may vary in the tourist areas, so always check your chosen restaurant.

Ventas – an excellent opportunity to eat reasonably priced meals almost any time of the day or night. These are motorway or roadside service areas. Often attached to a petrol station they are popular with lorry drivers and coach tours. There is usually a shop where you can buy local bread, veg and meat. And if you're lucky home made sausages.

Menu del Día – Though not usually very exciting, this fixed price meal is required of restaurants. It's a great way to taste some standard Spanish food, without the worry of a long menu. The prices for a menu del día almost always include bread, water and wine or beer, with a coffee at the end. They are very good value.

Menu – The principal ingredients of local Murcian dishes are the fresh produce of the Huerta (market garden – the fields of Murcia) and rice, fish and seafood from the nearby Mar Menor and the Mediterranean Sea.

Excellent choices are the king prawns and the "huevas de mújol" which is a local variety of caviar. The region also produces fine wines among which the most known are Jumilla and Yecla.

Eating Like A Spaniard

You may have noticed that Spanish restaurants seem awfully quiet…
…when you go in. This is probably because you haven't worked out
how to eat like a Spaniard yet. Read on to find out how to go native
and eat like a Spaniard and understand how military–precision timing
can be all–important (doesn't sound like Spain, does it?)

BREAKFAST

First Breakfast: in Spain, most people actually have two breakfasts.
The first breakfast is to get yourself started. Since most Spaniards start
the day early, the constitution is only ready to receive something light
at this stage – around 7:30. So first breakfast usually comprises any of
the following:

- Brandy (not necessarily a small one)
- Coffee (typically a milky one for breakfast)
- *Micocho* (a sponge cake often home made
  ("casero") – rather like Madeira cake)
- *Costillas* (not pork chops! – a thin, sugar–crusted
  cake with a fruit jam layer)
- *Pastel* (a large, fresh pastry or a pre–packaged,
  long–life cake (the last choice))

Second Breakfast is akin to elevenses
and is usually around 10–10:30.
These are typically very social affairs
and rather more substantial than the
first breakfast. If you go into a bar at

> *"Is it time for second breakfast
> yet?"* Pippin – The Lord of
> the Rings.

this time in the morning you may find it difficult to hear yourself
think. Second breakfast will comprise any of the following:

- Brandy (not necessarily a small one)
- Beer or red wine (white wine is a woman's drink
  (according to ever–so–slightly chauvinist Spanish men))
- Tapas (no holding back here, could be anything
  from tortilla to testicles)
- *Bocadillo*
- *Orujo* from the freezer to finish

The second breakfast sets you up nicely to last through to lunch as you spend the rest of the morning operating heavy machinery, driving an HGV, approving planning permissions, etc.

LUNCH

Lunch is eaten late. If you turn up at a restaurant and ask to eat at 12:30, you can expect slow service and a limited menu that may comprise left–over tapas from second breakfast. The majority of Spaniards start lunch at 2–2:30 (possibly an hour later at weekends). In fact, if you want to eat at some of the most popular restaurants, you'd be advised to turn up at about 1:45 unless you have reserved a table in advance – at 2:30 the place will be heaving. Like second breakfast, lunch is often eaten out at a restaurant with work colleagues during the week. At weekends, lunch is an opportunity to catch up with extended family – you'll usually see three generations (or more!) at the table.

During the week (and at other times in holiday areas), you will be able to get a *menú del día* – a set menu at a very reasonable price that includes drink (where "drink" could mean water, beer or house wine), salad, three courses and a coffee (which may include brandy, if that's what you fancy).

Spaniards typically don't have tapas at lunchtime. Lunchtime is the main meal of the day, to fill up and take your time (in order to help you feel sleepy enough for a few minutes' siesta afterwards).

At weekends the same establishment that served you a good–value, inexpensive *menú del díá* during the

Be aware of the word *menú* here – this is a 'false friend' – when you ask for the *'menu por favor'*, expecting to get the list of things to eat, the waiter will probably say *'¡si!'* and walk off, and start bringing you food that you didn't order. The thing is, you *did* just order – you ordered the fixed–price set menu (*menú del día*). You wanted the *carta*.

week will pull out all the stops and serve you an a la carta meal that will cost you twice as much for the "same thing". The difference is that the cut of meat will be better quality and twice the size, the wine will be better and the desserts more varied.

A typical lunchtime meal has the following:

- Brandy
- Salad (even in the depths of winter)
- A starter that is frequently larger than the second course. Starters include: soup (*consomé con albóndigas con un pocito fino* is one of our favourites), stew (*guiso*), pasta or rice (*arroz / paella*).
- The second course is usually something like meat / fish / eggs plus chips plus a grilled pepper.
- Dessert can include fruit or a pudding. Puddings to look out for are *casero* (home made): *flan* (crème caramel), *arroz con leche* (rice pudding) and *pan de calatrava* (crème caramel with a thin sponge base).
- Coffee (frequently without so much or any milk at this stage – *carajillo, bel monte or cortado* are usual)
- *Orujo* from the freezer to finish

SUPPER

Supper during the week is usually eaten at home with the family, at any time between 8 and 10. At weekends (starting Friday), suppertime is tapas time. This evening meal is (yet another) time to socialise, chat, flirt and speak very loudly.

Eating tapas (they even have a verb for it – *tapear*) requires you to do a bar crawl. Although lots of alcohol will be consumed over the course of the evening, it will always be accompanied with some food. This is why it is very unusual to see Spanish people drunk – in fact appearing drunk is very 'bad form' in Spain. The only exception to this rule might be at fiestas – then the booze flows freely!

Eating and drinking and drinking and eating – these activities are inseparable in Spain. A bartender will be shocked if you order so much as a *caña* (small glass of beer) without something to eat, even if something to eat is only a handful of olives.

The Spanish might not take timing seriously for anything else, but for food and drink, timing is important. If you don't want to stick out like a sore thumb, get there at the right time and eat and drink the right things. Soon enough you'll know all the waiters and bar staff by their first names and they'll have 'your usual' ready before you even get to the bar. *¡Te aproveche!*

Tapas Guide

"Tapas" are snacks designed to be served with your drink. It's widely believed that the name comes from the custom of the barman covering your glass of sherry with a slice of bread, cheese, or salami to keep the flies from drinking too much – "tapar" means to cover in Spanish.

However research suggests that the King Alfonso X el Sabio, who is said to have refused to serve his glorious wine to visitors unless they also had something to eat, introduced the term – he would "tapaba" them.

Madrid is probably the best known "tapas" destination, but the tradition is observed in many parts – especially in the southern half of the country. There are two approaches to tapas: one is a "freebie", a mouthful that comes with the price of your drink (often called a "pincho"). The second is a side–order snack purchased to accompany your glass of local wine.

It can be confusing at first, is this a free tapas, or will the price be added to your bill? Generally, if the waiter passes you a small plate of something, it's usually free. If they ask if you'd like something, then you will most likely pay.

Spaniards go to bars to chat, meet friends, argue, joke and flirt. Tapas are provided to keep them going and encourage the sales of drinks. Tapas are rarely eaten instead of a main meal but are good for soaking up the wine. Some of the best tapas bars can be found by universities and where commuters might congregate. This makes Murcia city a haven of tapas, especially around the Plaza de las Flores and Plaza Santa Catalina.

Each region has it's own specialities; in fact each bar also has its own favourites. Here is a selection you might meet (or eat!):

Jamón – ham off the bone, cut to order in almost all bars and restaurants. You'll see the leg on a special holder at the bar and often you'll see many legs hanging from the ceiling (with their little upside down umbrellas to catch the fat). The Jamón is taken seriously in Spain, with a number of varieties including Iberico, Serrano and Bellota.

Patatas Alioli – Boiled potatoes, in a creamy Alioli sauce (raw garlic mayonnaise) topped with a sprinkle of parsley.

Patatas Bravas – Potatoes with a hot mustard, tomato and Tabasco sauce.

Tortilla – A fat omelette made with potatoes which sometimes includes peas, meat, tuna, peppers or mushrooms.

Magras con Tomate – Fried pork cooked in a sweet tomato sauce.

Calamares – Fried, beautifully fresh calamari, that melts in your mouth and Calamares en su tinta, squid in their own ink

Aceitunas or Olivas– Olives – big, fat olives, often with stalks intact, firm to bite.

Pollo al Ajillo con Vino – Garlic chicken with wine

Caldo en Albóndigas – Meatballs in a watery soup (consommé)

Gazpacho – Cold tomato soup, almost like a salad, only usually available in the summer, unfortunately!

Local Food Specialities

Revuelto – Revuelto is a common name for another tapas counter staple – eggs scrambled with runner beans, garlic, onions and ham.

Zarangollo – Zarangollo is a Murcian dish combining the concepts of ratatouille and omelette. It is made from tomatoes, courgettes, onions and eggs. Every tapas bar worth its salt in the region should have a plateful in the chiller. Menestra is similar, a dish of sautéed vegetables

Ensalada Murciana – A wet salad of cooked red peppers and tomatoes, garlic, aubergine and onions. Always served cold and frequently with some fish (tuna or cod) thrown in. Almost always on the tapas counter.

Pastel de carne – Little pasty or pie shaped pastries, filled with delicious meat, tomato and egg. Very good, give it a try. These are often bought to take to the Condomina bullring in Murcia, where they always have a merienda (snack) after the 3rd bull.

Arroz – Rice is grown in the Calasparra region, with it's own quality standards.

Among the wide variety of rice dishes are:

- Arroz y conejo – rice with rabbit
- Arroz de verduras – rice and vegetables
- Arroz y costillejas – rice and ribs
- Arroz marinero – seafood rice
- Paella huertana – a vegetable paella

Potaje – a rich stew dish

Habas con jamón – ham and broad beans

Caldo murciano – local soup dish

Michirones – a spicy bean stew with pork and saussage (usually eaten with a toothpick)

Chuletas al ajo cabañil – garlic chops

Pescado a la sal – baked fish in salt

Fresh Vegetables & Fruit – Known as the market garden (huerta), the Murcia region boasts an extensive and year round fruit and veg selection. Many of the fruit and vegetables you'll find in supermarkets in the UK will have come from Murcia – particularly tomatoes, melons and oranges.

Wild Boar – Jabalí is available as a delicacy throughout Spain, and Murcia is no exception. The boar is served in a number of dishes (including the famous wild boar with figs) as well as just roasted.

Cheeses – The best cheeses in Murcia are granted a DOC rating, just like the wines of Yecla, Jumilla and Bullas. There are two categories of the Murcia DOC cheese, 'Queso de Murcia' and 'Queso de Murcia al Vino'. The Murcia DOC cheeses are all produced from whole milk from Murciano–Granadina goats.

The 'Queso de Murcia' DOC comes in two varieties, fresh and semi–cured. The fresh variety is mild, white and has a woven texture on the rind from the tall, cylindrical mold. The cured variety is cured for at least 60 days, is rather more flavoured with a firmer texture, some holes and a smooth rind.

The 'Queso de Murcia al Vino' DOC is a richer cheese with a characteristic reddish colour which comes from the wine that the cheese is soaked in while maturing. The cheese is matured for at least 45 days for large moulds, and 30 days for smaller cheeses.

Caviar – A locally–produced variant of caviar (huevas de mújol) is produced on the Mar Menor. It's available in jars in most local supermarkets at a very reasonable price compared to 'the real thing' – but tastes pretty good!

For a whole list of Murcian recipes (in Spanish) go to:

http://canales.laverdad.es/gastronomia/murcianas.htm

And for some in English

www.spain.info/TourSpain/Gastronomia/Cocina+Regional/CCAA/Q/0/R++Murcia.htm

Vegetarians

Being a vegetarian in Murcia can sometimes be a little challenging. Local culture celebrates the pig and ham as a staple food, to be consumed at every opportunity. Here is a list of the top 3 vegetarian options:

Revueltos – scrambled eggs, you could ask for them with mushrooms – setas or with asparagus – espárrago. Remember to specify "sin jamón" to have a better chance of having scrambled eggs without the ubiquitous ham!

Patatas Bravas or Patatas Alioli – potataoes with spicy hot sauce or garlic mayonnaise.

Huevos con patatas – egg and chips!

SIN CARNE?

When ordering for a vegetarian friend in a long–established restaurant in Murcia, we ordered the safe option – revueltos 'sin carne'. When it arrived we had to explain that even the little bits of ham in the eggs weren't appetising to our friend and asked if they wouldn't mind starting again without meat, and without jamón.

Local Drinks

Asiático – The Asiático variant of coffee is a speciality of the Campo de Cartagena. It's made from coffee, condensed milk, Spanish brandy, a liqueur called Licor 43, a pair of coffee beans, (optional) sugar and a sprinkle of cinnamon powder. In the best bars you will get a tiny wedge of lemon zest and it will be served in the 'original' glass – a miniature, vase–shaped, ornate affair resembling a milkshake glass.

The drink was created in a bar in El Albujón (a small town just north of Cartagena) called Bar Pedrín – according to legend, the drink was originally called a 'ruso' but was changed to 'asiático' during Franco's times since a communist drink was not exactly flavour of the moment.

Belmonte – You will notice the locals in Murcia most often drink a strange coffee concoction called a Belmonte. It comprises a good shot of condensed milk (more often than not from a special dispenser mounted by the coffee machine), followed by a shot of café solo and finished off with a shot (or two) of Spanish brandy.

BELMONTES

Possibly the most versatile drink in the world. Taken after dinner as a digestif, the brandy bottle is always left for regulars to add an extra slosh, to swill down the coffee and clean out the glass (just to help with the washing up, of course). Taken after lunch, it's a great way to induce the siesta and taken at breakfast to warm the blood, you'll find

office workers, doctors, truck drivers and policemen enjoying
its healthy properties.

Orujo – Orujo is not a speciality of Murcia (it's principally from
Galicia, actually) but that doesn't put the locals off from drinking it
fairly liberally after meals. This digestif comes in a number of varieties,
from the plain (a colourless, 40 percent spirit), to a wide variety of
flavoured varieties of a lower strength. Local favourite flavourings are
coffee and herbs.

Wine Guide

There are two classifications of Murcian wine: Vinos de la Tierra and
in Murcia these are from Abanilla and Campo de Cartagena; and
DOC, which implies that the wine only comes from a particular area,
with a particular set of grapes and that the conditions of production
are controlled.

The DOC (Denominación de Origen) wine region encompasses
Jumilla, Bullas and Yecla. It gets incredibly hot here in the summer,
which inevitably raises the sugar levels in the grapes. The higher the
sugar levels the higher the alcohol content. For many years the wines
of this region were strong and heavy and mainly exported to other
regions for blending. However, cooperatives are persuading the
growers to develop new ways of working that are producing some very
drinkable and attractive wines.

Red wine grapes are Monastrell, Granache (Garnacha), Tempranillo,
Cabernet Sauvignon, Merlot and Shiraz (Syrah).

White wine grapes are Airén and Macabeo.

Jumilla

In particular Jumilla wines are making an impact in the UK. The
Jumilla DOC comes from a number of towns: Jumilla, Montealegre del
Castillo, Albatana, Ontur, Hellín and Tobarra. They produce a number
of varieties, the king of these being the Monastrell grape.

To the north of the Murcia region, there are many bodegas selling top
quality Reds, Whites and Rosados.

Bullas

The north west of the region is an upcoming wine producing area supported by the European Vinest Project. The wine is produced in the towns of Mula, Calasparra, Ricote, Caravaca, Cehegín, Moratalla, Lorca and Bullas itself.

OUR FAVOURITES

We adore the Carrascalejo wine. Carrascalejo produce some bright rosados, which seem to go well with any meal. They are light and fruity with strawberry and raspberry flavours. Their Tinto Crianza is a great "upmarket" wine, costing a shocking €4 per bottle when bought at the Bodega (about €5 in the supermarkets), which goes very well with stronger meats and cheeses.

From Casa Bernal (*http://casabernal.com*) Casa Bernal – c/ Mayor, 90, 30120–El Palmar–Murcia tel. 34 + 68 884304 – you can get a fantastic yearly list of their top 12 Wines (Taberna De Los 12 Vinos). All wines are selected for their interest and quality, and if you like wine, these are a good place to start. This is also the name of their excellent restaurant, which is surprisingly quiet.

We have been unable to find a really good local white wine. So we usually buy a Rueda such as a Martivillí.

Yecla

In the far north east of the region, neighbouring Jumilla, the Yecla wines are only produced in the local region around the town itself and characterised by a more subtle balance between strength and acidity.

Campo de Cartagena

Bodegas Serrano in the Finca La Cabaña 30, 30594 Pozo Estrecho, Cartagena (Murcia) ☎968 55 62 98. The owners are Manuel Martinez Meroño and his wife Carmen Inglés Inglés. Sampling these wines is quite an experience. The wine doesn't have its DO, however, there are some lovely Reds and Rosados, quite subtle.

FOOD & DRINK CHEAT SHEET	
Comedor	Dining room
Carta	Menu
Menú del día	Fixed price menu
Comida or Almuerzo	Lunch
La cuenta	The bill
Platos combinados	Mixed plate
Cucharra	Spoon
Cuchillo	Knife
Tenedor	Fork
Vaso/Copa	Glass
Taza	Cup
Camerero/Camerera	Waiter/Waitres
Cena	Dinner
Desayuno	Breakfast
Frío	Cold
Caliente	Hot
Hielo	Ice
Entradas	**Starters**
Sopa	Soup
Sopa de cocido	Meat soup
Sopa de gallina	Chicken soup

Ensalada	Salad
Ensalada Mixta	Mixed salad
Aceitunas or Olivas	Olives
Primeros Platos	**Main Courses**
A la plancha	Grilled
A la brasa	Grilled
A la parilla	Grilled
Al horno	Baked/Roasted
Crudo	Raw
Asado	Roasted
Frito	Fried
Cocido/caldereta	Stew
Arroz	Rice
Paella	Famous rice dish
Verduras	Vegetables
Patatas	Potatos
Patatas Fritas	Chips
Judias	Green beans
Zanahorias	Carrots
Guisantes	Peas
Ajo (al ajillo)	Garlic (in garlic)
Tomates	Tomatoes
Pimientos rojos	Red Peppers

Pimientos verdes	Green Pepers
Pollo	Poultry
Pato	Duck
Pavo	Turkey
Pechuga	Breast of poultry
Perdiz	Partridge
Pollo	Chicken
Carne	Meat
Cabra/chivo	Goat/baby goat
Caza	Game
Cerdo	Pork
Cochinillo	Suckling pig
Conejo	Rabbit
Cordero	Lamb
Solomillo	Fillet Steak
Entrecot	Sirloin Steak
Lomo	Pork loin
Ternera	Beef, veal
Pescado	Fish
Dorada	Sea Bream
Atún	Tuna
Anchoa/boquerones	Anchovy
Bacalao	Salted cod

Lenguado	Sole
Emperador	Swordfish
Mojama	Cured tuna
Mariscos	Shellfish
Gambas	Prawns
Mejillones	Mussels
Almejas	Clams
Langostinos	Crayfish
Langostas/Bogavante	Lobster
Postres	**Desserts**
Helado de Chocolate	Chocolate ice cream
Helado de Vainilla	Vanilla ice cream
Tarta	Flan / Cake
Flan	Crème Caramel
Frutas	Fruit
Manzanas	Apples
Naranjas	Oranges
Uvas	Grapes
Ciruelas	Plums
Melocotones	Peaches
Cerezas	Cherries
Fresas	Strawberries
Piña	Pineapple

Plátanos	Bananas
Bebidas	**Drinks**
Vino Tinto	Red Wine
Vino Blanco	White Wine
Cerveza	Beer
Zumo de naranja	Orange juice
Agua	Water
Zumo de Manzana	Apple juice
Sangria	Red wine spritzer with fruit juice
Tinto de verano	Red wine spritzer
Alimento General	**General Food**
Aceite	Oil
Ajo	Garlic
Arroz	Rice
Azúcar	Sugar
Huevos	Eggs
Mantequilla	Butter
Miel	Honey
Pan	Bread
Pimienta	Pepper
Sal	Salt
Vinagre	Vinegar
Salsa	Sauce

Towns

Ayuntamiento: The town hall in Spain is called the 'Ayuntamiento'. While this is a bit of a tounge–twister, it's well worth learning since just about *everything* to do with officialdom revolves around your local ayuntamiento. From registering to vote (empadronar) which in turn enables you to register your car and ask Telefónica for a new telephone line, to making planning applications for a patio (yes, patios need planning permission in Spain) – you will have to involve the ayuntamiento.

Fortunately, for many things, you can get a gestor to do the job for you, and this will save you a *lot* of time in queues and frustration trying to find the right department.

Here is a directory with addresses and telephone numbers:

www.guiadeayuntamientos.info

Correos: The post office in Spain is called the 'Correos' and has signs in bright yellow. The larger towns will have PO boxes ('apartado de correos') for rent for around €40 a year which is useful for those who have a place out in the sticks where the postie on his/her little yellow Vespa fears to travel to. It should be pointed out that the Spanish postal system isn't as good as the UK (even these days, no, really!) and post even within the country often takes more than a week to arrive and frequently disappears.

Plaza Mayor: Almost every town has a central square, and it's almost invariably called 'Plaza Mayor'. While there are some curious exceptions where Plaza Mayor isn't actually the best–known square in the town (such as in Murcia itself). The most useful aspect of the Plaza Mayor is as a meeting place – eg to meet the builders or delivery drivers who don't know where your house is in the village. Also you will get some vans making weekly deliveries of bottled drinks and Repsol gas passing through the Plaza Mayor.

Teleclub: The town and village senior citizen's club (Salon de Mayores) is sponsored by the Ayuntamiento and is often referred to as the 'teleclub' (on account of the clubs being one of the first places to have TV's in villages in days gone by). Some villages don't have any bar as such, but *do* have a teleclub. Sometimes they are rather hard to find (no garish neon signs) but there will always be one… somewhere. You don't really have to be a member to use the facilities, although it's very 'Good Form' to enrol as a member of your local; it only costs a few Euros and you don't have to be a pensioner! You will find that village meals for Christmas, Easter and other fiestas will be held here, along with a healthy Sunday pre–lunch crowd, often with caldo de albóndigas (meatballs in consommé – best with a dash of fino sherry into the bowl) from the pot.

CHATS WITH THE BOYS

The Spanish way of life, and what we've been searching for, includes making the time to chat. Whether it's in the market, on a bench or in the teleclub, chatting is a national pastime. On many occasions, Marcus has sat with our neighbours, David and Joaquín, chatting until the sun sets. They'll drink a little wine or beer, eat a few nuts, and sort out some of the world's most pressing problems. Like the debate between fascists and capitalists, how immigration is affecting the economy or how many kilos of olives you can expect per tree.

Turismo: The tourist information offices (the 'i') in Spain are called the 'Oficina de Turismo', or simply 'el turismo'. Their usefulness varies wildly from town to town, some handing out just one leaflet (after you have persuaded the council employee to stop chatting on their mobile for a minute) through to ones that will deluge you with information. At the very least you should be able to get a free town plan here. Don't expect the turismo to be open on Sunday or during siesta time.

Jenkins

Guide

✈   Airport

☎   Telephone number

ⓘ   Tourist information

★   Hotel classifications

The prices for hotels are for one room with 2 people sharing unless otherwise stated.

We have included a Map Reference for all major towns. This includes the grid reference for the map found on the following page.

VALENCIA

Yecla

Jumilla

Sierra del Carche

To Valencia

Sierra de la Pila

Alicante

Fortuna

Archena

ula

Murcia

El Valle

La Murta

Lo Pagán

San Pedro del Pinatar

San Javier

Santiago de la Ribera

Carrascoy

Los Alcázares

Mar Menor

Fuente Álamo

La Manga

Cabo de Palos

olnuevo

Mazarrón

Cartagena

Calblanque

Puerto Mazarrón

Calnegre

Mediterranean

as

D   E   F

Águilas

Population: 28,000

Map Reference: C1 1.57°W, 37.40°N

This southwestern city near the Murcian coast has an arid and mountainous landscape, extensive beaches with crystalline cliffs and small, little frequented coves.

The hill where the Castle of San Juan of the Águilas is based (century XVIII) was a refuge to a population afraid of pirate attacks. Its dilapidated condition prevents access to the interior, but it offers an excellent viewpoint of the town and the surrounding coast.

There's the Museum Arqueologico and Centro de Interpretacion del Mar, in the centre of town. A stroll to the Port, dominated by the lighthouse, leads to the wholesale fish market, where at 5pm there's a fish auction.

To see the natural splendour of the region is the main reason for visiting. If you travel on from the beach at Poniente, you reach a group of coves – Cuatro Calas. These are in a protected area and so are not only great places for quiet sunbathing but also good for walks.

Tranquil beaches with fine sand, huge cliffs and beautiful coves can be found at San Pedro, Blanca and Los Hierros. Los Hierros is dominated by the tower named Torre De Cope, which has been attacked on numerous occasions by pirates. Close by are the beach at Calabardina and the natural park of Calnegre–Cabo Cope.

In February you can enjoy Carnaval, which has a Rio de Janeiro feel about it, with 3 days and nights of floats, processions and fancy dress.

ⓘ Tourist Office – Plaza Antonio Cortijos
☎ 968 493285
www.aguilas.org
www.aguilas.tv

Ayuntamiento
www.ayuntamientodeaguilas.org
☎ 968 418800

Taxis

☎ 968 411 470 – Calles Isaac Peral

☎ 968 410 149 – Munoz Calero

Buses – stop at the bar on the corner of Avenida Juan Carlos 1 and Calle Carlos Marín Menú. Buses go to Almería, Cartagena, Lorca and Murcia.

There are trains to Murcia and Lorca, with 3 daily trains to each.

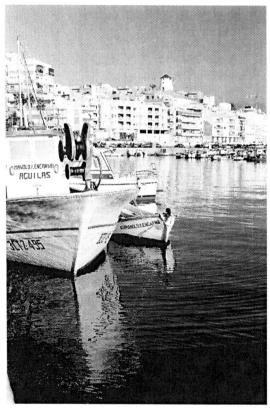

Harbour at Águilas

Where To Sleep

There is a wide range of accommodation which includes camping in Aguilas (☎968 419205) and Bellavista (☎968 449151). Prices rise by about €12 in summer. Remember in summer and during fiestas you must make reservations well ahead of arrival.

Hotel El Paso ★ ★ ★
Calle Cartagena, 13
A/C, TV
42 – 54 Euros per night
☎   968 447125

Hotel El Paraíso ★ ★
Ctra. Cabo Cope–Calabardina
A/C, TV, Near the beach of Calabardina.
40 – 51 Euros per night
☎   968 419447

Hotel Al Sur ★ ★ ★
Torre de Cope, 24 – Calabardina
Small but pricey, good sea views and nice location
60 – 93 Euros per night
☎   968 419466

Pensión Águileña
Calle Isabel Católica, 8
Cheap, basic and central
☎   968 410303

Pensión Rodríguez
Calle Ramon
☎   968 410615

Hotel Carlos III
Calle Rey Carlos III, 22
☎   968 411650
www.hotelcarlosiii.com

Night Life

In summer there are a lot of bars, discos and ice cream parlours ("heladerías") along the beach front, especially recommended are Mar Azul and Colonia. The centre of the town has a number of pubs and bars, a lot of which have terraces. In the early hours of the morning the night life gets busy around the Plaza de España. Good night spots include La Glorieta, Dakota, Bhudabú and Tuareg.

Where To Eat

Águilas is a great place to eat fish and seafood, including prawns, octopus and sea bass.

- Las Brisas – Explanada del Puerto –rich paella and fried fish.
- El Faro – Calle José María Pereda – typical local dishes at reasonable prices, menu €15.
- Rey Carlos III – calle Rey Carlos III, 22 –good fish and seafood.
- Café Bar La Cigarrera – Calle Aire, 78. On the beach, specialises in fish and seafood including battered squid.
- Café Bar La Poza – Avenida Juan Carlos I, 10. Roast octopus and anchovies in vinegar.
- Café Bar Felipe – Plaza Alfonso Escámez, 1. Has a nice terrace for people watching. Dried octopus, prawns, and mixed fried fish.
- Café Bar Mónaco – Calle Méndez Núñez. Very near the beach with Pulpo a la Gallega (Galician style octopus) as the speciality of the house.
- Café Bar Peña Aguilera – Avenida Juan Carlos I, 17. This bar offers some delicacies that are for the more adventurous, such as snails, baby squid and some more challenging meat dishes like morcilla (Spanish black pudding).
- Café Bar Rincón Maravillas – Calle Ramón y Cajal, 2. Caracoles, traditional Spanish cuts of pork (including trotters).
- Casa Pepe – Calle Muñoz Calero. Good selection of grilled tapas including kebabs on skewers (Pinchos or Pinchos Morunas).
- Café Bar Sol Y Mar – Plaza Antonio Cortijos. Outside seating with the usual variety of seafood.
- ¡N! La Veleta – Calle Blas Rosique, 6. Good but pricey.

- Pescados Submarino – Calle Isaac Peral, 3. Battered squid.
- Taberna Típica El Pimiento – Calle Joaquín Tendero. Meat–lovers only: snails, fried rabbit, fried liver and black pudding.

Alhama De Murcia

Population: 16,400

Map Reference: D3 1.42°W, 37.85°N

The Arabs built a castle to defend Alhama (which the Arabs called Alhamman) where the thermal waters made famous by the Romans can be found. Today Alhama is a city with fruit in the valleys and pines on the mountains lying at the foothills of the Sierra Espuña.

The Ayuntamiento is an early 20th century building in the Plaza de la Constitución. There are a number of parks in the centre near the ancient house, Casa De La Familia Saavedra. Nearby is the Iglesia de la Concepción, which is a Baroque church restored in the 18th century

In Plaza Vieja at the end of Calle Larga there are some 19th century stately houses with brightly coloured facades and the old town hall, which houses the museum (open week days – closed for siesta).

You can go up to the Arab castle using side streets off Calle Vergara. In the same area you will find the baroque Iglesia de san Lázaro. Also nearby you'll find the famous bathhouses of the town.

ⓘ Tourist Office – Plaza de La Constitución
Open every day apart from Sundays and during siesta.
☎ 968 633512

Ayuntamiento
www.paralelo40.org/alhama
You can arrive by train on the Aguilas – Murcia line and also the Lorca – Barcelona line.
Taxis – Tomás Moro
☎968 630063 ☎968 639143 ☎968 630728

Where To Sleep
Hotel Entresierras ★ ★ ★
Autovía E15, km 642, Librilla
This is the best accommodation in the area! All mod–cons, but it is 13km from Alhama. €55 per night for a double room
☎   968 659110

Hotel Los Bartolos ★ ★
Calle Alfonso X el Sabio, 1
Modern hotel with A/C & TV, often full during the week.
€40 per night
☎   968 631671

Where To Eat
Specialties are rice / paella with rabbit, snails and migas.

- Filipinas Casa El Lobo – Ctra Cartagena, km 58 – Popular homemade food.
- Los Bartolos – Calle Alfonso X El Sabio, 1 – one of the best quality restaurants, with good fish and local specialities.
- Julian – Ctra N340 – Restaurant and bar which has hearty food at a good price and is very popular with local workers.
- El Chaleco – Avenida Bastarreche, 9 – high quality restaurant, specialising in fish and desserts. Slightly more pricey.

Nightlife
In summer everyone goes to Mazarrón, however the rest of the year you'll find people in the city. 'Twenty–somethings' will probably like the Virgina in Calle de Gil. A more rowdy bar is Ruta on Calle Vidal Abarca, a large place, open all night. Another bar to try is Nifas y Faunos on calle Corredera. Avenida Ginés Campos also has many bars and clubs.

Archena

Population: 15,000

Map Reference: D4 1.29°W, 38.11°N

Archena can be found on the last natural part of the Río Segura, before it heads into the city (Murcia). Archena is used as a base for visiting the Balneario de Archena and also for walks and excursions up the Valle De Ricote.

Balneario Archena

Balneario is based about 2km from the centre of Archena, where there are a number of hotels and pleasant walks along the Rio de Segura. The thermal baths at Balneario have therapeutic properties, with temperatures around 50° centigrade.

The Balneario website is not too great, promising an English translation – however it disappoints! This shouldn't stop you from visiting Balneario though – which is superb. Prices for the baths are around €5.50 for 3 hours during weekdays, with €1 per extra hour. During the weekends and fiestas prices increase to €8.50 for 3 hours and €2 per additional hour.

It was recently expanded and is even better value, with a multitude of jets, whirlpools and jacuzzis.

Balneario offers between 2 and 14 day intensive programs of therapeutic remedies and relaxation.

There is also an 18th century church – Iglesia de San Juan Bautista.
☎ 902 366 902
www.balnearioarchena.com

Ayuntamiento on Calle Major
☎ 968 670 000

Buses to and from Murcia can be found in Avenida del Carril. Also you can get the bus from here to Balneario.

Taxi rank in Plaza Primero de Mayo
☎ 968 670 044

Where To Sleep

Hotel Levante ★ ★ ★ ★
In Baleario de Archena
Luxury hotel with good views to the gardens. €80 per night.
☎   968 670 100
www.balneario–archena–sa.es
Hotel La Parra ★
Ctra Los Banos, 2
Family style accommodation which is more economical. €40 for a double room.
☎   968 670 444

Hotel León ★ ★ ★
In Balneario de Archena
A/C, swimming pool, €80, Good restaurant, but pricey.
☎   968 670 100

Hotel Termas ★ ★ ★ ★
In Balneario de Archena
Upmarket hotel, with prices to match. €102 per night for a double room
Good restaurant, but pricey.
☎   968 670 100

Where To Eat

- Gamba de Oro – Calle Juan José Marco Benegas – tapas bar specialising in seafood which is very popular at weekends.
- Bar José – Avenida del Carril – famous tapas bar with high quality seafood, ham and cheeses.
- Mesón Las Minas – Pedanía de la Algaida – generous portions of local tapas.
- El Internacional – Ctra. del Balneario – modern, functional restaurant with a terrace.
- Madrid – Calle Juan José Marco Benegas – excellent home made cooking.
- El Triunfo – Ctra. del Balneario, 4 – specialises in paellas and has a nice terrace.

Night Life

In Archena itself there are a number of options – a trendy bar with music is La Fuente in La Plaza Primero de Mayo. Bars with terraces are El Practicante and Jardín in Calle Alejandro Medina. Other bars to try include Pop'rron, La Posada and Renta, which are all near Calle Argentina.

In Balneario de Archena you shouldn't miss the Bar Azul, which is a pleasant place to pass an evening with a giant chess set amongst the palm trees on the terrace with a medley of cats around your feet.

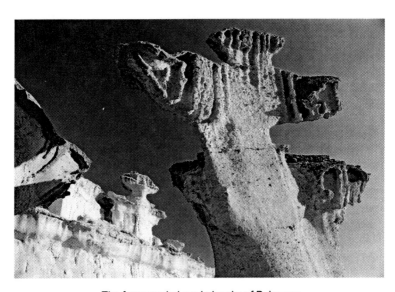

The famous wind eroded rocks of Bolnuevo

Bolnuevo

Population: 260

Map Reference: D1 1.31°W, 37.56°N

An upmarket seaside resort near Puerto Mazarrón. Bolneuvo has one of the most recognisable landmarks of Murcia – the weathered sandstone formation that adorns most of the region's brochures and tourist guides.

Following the coast road to the south west brings you to miles of beautiful, and often secluded coves and beaches, including a number of nudist spots. The road is very narrow and pitted so keep your wits about you as it's mostly only wide enough for one car.

Carrying on further towards Águilas, you reach Punta Calnegre, where there are more organised beaches, with a family orientation. These are best reached by car from the Mazarrón – Águilas road.

Bullas

Population: 11,000

Map Reference: C3 1.66°W, 38.05°N

Bullas is one of the five regions which makes up the area called Comarca del Noroeste – the natural access to the north east of the region.

The first Sunday of every month on Plaza Vieja (until lunchtime) there is a comprehensive market, selling not only the usual fare of fruit, veg and dodgy watches, but also local arts and crafts, including ceramics and wood carvings.

Their fiesta is in October, starting the night of the Friday before the first Sunday of October and finishing on the following Tuesday. There is also a fiesta on the 17th January, San Antón (La Copa).

Ayuntamiento – Plaza de España

☎   968 652031

www.bullas.net – this is one of the best local websites in the region, perhaps in the whole of Spain! You'll find a lot of tourist information on this site too.

Where To Sleep

Camping – Complejo de La Rafa, E–30180–Bullas–Murcia,

☎   968 654 666

www.campinglarafa.com

Take a look on *www.noratur.com* for other places.

Where To Eat

- Restaurante Avenida Avda. de Murcia, 19 – Specialities include seafood, fish and sirloin.
- Restaurante–Bar Fernández Avda. Luis de los Reyes, 7 – Homemade cooking and various tapas.
- Restaurante Flipper Avda. de Murcia, 48 – Paella and roast chicken.
- Restaurante La Rafa Camping La Rafa – Local cooking.
- Restaurante–Bar Mateo Avda de Murcia, 77 – Meat, fish and various tapas.
- Restaurante Polideportivo Avda. de Murcia – Meat, fish and various tapas.
- Restaurante–Bar Las Peñas Calle Nicolás de las Peñas, 56 – Roast octopus, fish and meat.
- Restaurante Molino de Abajo Ctra. Bullas–Totana Km. 2 – Local specialities.

Cabo de Palos

Population: 550

Map Reference: F2 0.70°W, 37.63°N

Across from the Marchamalo salt flats, Cabo de Palos is a small point of land jutting out into the Mediterranean. Naturally equipped with many small bays and inlets, it has always been a centre for fishing and the main port area is one of the prettiest on the entire coast. Using fresh local fish and vegetables, some of the best restaurants in the area line the traditional quayside and offer very reasonable prices.

This is a marina town with a famous lighthouse up on the hill, from where you can expect to have great seafood. A heaving, trendy place in the summer, visit off–season to enjoy the food. But beware, in off–season many of the restaurants close.

Where To Eat

- Restaurante Natana – Paseo de la Barra – a quayside place with fish and rice specialty.
- Mesón el Mosqui – on the way up to the lighthouse. One of the really good "caldero" rice places in the area. Closes Thursdays.
- Restaurante el Pez Roco – Paseo de la Barra – Balcony over the port. Good fish.
- Miramar – Paseo de la Barra, 14 – excellent fresh fish
- Restaurante Miramar – Beginning of Paseo de la Barra.
- Restaurante El Navegante – End Paseo de La Barra, corner El Faro/Palangre Streets. Fish and rices.
- Restaurante La Sartenica – Tavern–Restaurant, in the way up to the Lighthouse, wide selection of typical Murcian snacks.
- Restaurante Kati – Fish and rice in the first bend of Way Up Road to the LightHouse.
- Restaurante Freiduría El Faro – Fried fish, in the port Avenue.
- Restaurante El Rape – Old La Manga – Cabo de Palos road, traffic lights cross in front of Las Dunas "mercadillo" – the Sunday morning flea market. Different caldero and paella rices, cod, ribsteaks.

- Restaurante La Tana – Paseo de la Barra (facing the entrance of the port) – Tradition in good fish and rices. Its dish "Rice La Tana" (a "caldero" type rice made with minced squids and shrimps, with no heads and no bones) is delicious.
  www.la–tana.com

Night Life

Cabo de Palos nightlife is tremendously full of activity and noise especially from Friday to Sunday and from June to September. There are a lot of places to go and drink, listen to music and dance, open from 11 pm to 4, 5 or 6 am. Then you can go somewhere else for breakfast!

There are several main areas where many of these music pubs are concentrated. Here are two of them.

Central Cabo de Palos – Most of the places here are located within the triangle made by three adjacent streets: Calle Salero, Calle Marín and Plaza de Los Arcos. You get there following the road that drives from the Port of Cabo de Palos to the Light House, just before reaching El Mosqui Restaurant.

Las Dunas – Many of the Disco–Bars in this area are in El Mercadillo building, old road La Manga–Cabo de Palos–Cartagena, when you find a cross road with traffic lights that follows down to the port of Cabo de Palos.

There is a lot of activity in summer, but in winter everything stops.

Calasparra

Population: 9,300

Map Reference: C4 1.70°W, 38.23°N

Noted for its excellent rice growing, which is due to the proximity of the rivers Segura, Quípar and Argos. In the centre of town you can find the remains of an Arab castle off Plaza de la Constitución. There is an archaeological museum in the old Palace House of La Encomienda, there are a number of old churches such as Iglesia de la Merced, Iglesia de san Pedro (18th century) and Iglesia de los Santos (18th century).

Calasparra specialities such as rice, sweets and cheeses can be found in Calle Teniente Flomesta.

Around Calasparra you can go up to Las Lomas de la Virgen to get a fantastic view of the mountains, the river and the rice fields. Nearby you'll find the natural reserve of Cañadaverosa. Another nearby beauty spot is Cañón de Los Almadenes.

Calasparra has a fiesta of Virgen de la Esperanza which is between the 2nd and 8th of September.

The Rice

Calasparra rice is the first in the world to have been awarded a "Denominación de Origen" – DOC, which symbolises a guarantee of high quality.

The rice is grown in a special environment – both sunny and mountainous, ranging from 340 to 500 metres in altitude, and irrigated with fresh water from the river Segura.

The cultivation uses a unique irrigation system, allowing the fresh water to be continually renewed. The clever use of crop rotation ensures the land is allowed to rest. The traditional seeds (Bomba and Balilla X Sollana) are almost unique to this region and are the only ones ever used.

The ripening process takes much longer than with other rice varieties (approx 30% longer) and this natural drying gives the rice a distinctive taste and texture. The grain is especially hard and Calasparra rice needs more water for cooking, which means the rice never sticks together and always looks fluffy!

The rice comes in sealed packs, often made from cotton, each one carrying a numbered label issued by the Consejo Regulador, guaranteeing its authenticity and quality.

You can buy the rice in most large supermarkets throughout the Murcian region and from shops in Calasparra and surrounds.

ⓘ Tourist Office – San Abdón, 15
☎   968 723000

Ayuntamiento – Plaza Corredera, 27
☎   968 720044
www.foro–ciudad.com/murcia/calasparra

Buses – the corner of Calle Teniente Flomesta.

Taxis – rank next to Iglesia de la Merced.

Train station – 4 km out to the north of town.

Where To Stay
B&B – Albergue Las Lomas – 1km from Santuario de Virgen de la Esperanza
Good views, 7 wooden cabins

Casa Rural – Palmera Moya
Old house with capacity for 6 to 8 people.
☎   968 746143

Camping
Los Viveros – in the area of Santuario de Virgen de la Esperanza

Where To Eat
Eating rice in Calasparra is just about compulsory! Try some of these good–value places:

- Las Lomas – Ctra del Santuario – modern restaurant with fantastic views and rich paellas (which you may need to pre–order).
- Soyma – Calle Teniente Flomesta, 15 – central restaurant with generous portions.
- Virgen de la Esperanza – Santuario de Virgen de la Esperanza – rich paellas mixtas are available on the fixed price menu.

Night Life
In the fiesta period Calasparra really shines with lots of live music especially in the Puberas (bar/club). A lot of the other bars have quite

a relaxed, sophisticated nature. Places to try include Titus, Pinver and Rialto which are on Calle Miguel Hernández. You'll also find some other bars in the area of Avenida Primero de Mayo and in Calle Germán Galindo.

Calblanque

Map Reference: F2 0.78°W, 37.62°N

Calblanque is a remote and almost untouched stretch of coast, just south of the Mar Menor. This designated natural park enjoys secluded bays, solitude and an abundance of wild birds and flowers. Boardwalks criss–cross the sand dunes leading down to the beaches, with paths along the coast.

Best reached by car access is via a bumpy road, off the main road to La Manga. The area is completely protected from the uncontrolled building which has affected other coastal destinations.

The beaches are great for scuba diving and snorkelling as the waters are very clear. You are more likely to bump into a herd of goats than see an armada of pedalos sailing past.

Caravaca De La Cruz

Population: 23,000

Map Reference: C4 1.86°W, 38.10°N

Caravaca de la Cruz is a beautiful medieval (12th and 13th century) town, with many historic, traditional properties in the old quarter. The town has been declared by the Vatican as one of the world's Holy Cities, along with Rome, Jerusalem, Santiago de Compostela and Santa Toribio de Liebana, thus giving Spain three out of five. Caravaca de la Cruz is also allowed to celebrate the Perpetual Jubilee once every seven years. The next time will be in 2010.

Narrow streets and alleys lead towards the castle, built in the 15th century and commissioned by the Knights Templar. Parking is a nightmare – park whereever you can find a space and walk! Once out and about, you'll quickly find a number of museums, such as Museo Sacro de la Vera Cruz (religious artefacts), Museo de los Festejos and also Museo Arqueológico.

Down in the centre of town the main attractions are the Iglesia del Salvador, the monastery at Iglesia de San José and Ermita de San Sebastián (with interesting murals). Around the area you can find the spring at Fuentes de Marqués and various archeological sites at Cueva Negra, Palacia de Armas, Los Villares, Cerro de la Ermitas and Cuevo del Rey Moro.

Up the hill, you'll find the most photographed church in the area, El Santuario de Vera Cruz, with a pink marble facade. The church houses the cross used in the Easter celebrations – Semana Santa.

At the beginning of May Caravaca has very famous and popular fiestas – Santísima y Vera Cruz. Book your accommodation well in advance.

Another popular part of the May fiesta is los Caballos del Vino (wine horses), in commemoration of a tradition that took place in the 13th century. The Christians besieged in the fortress by the Arabs managed to break the siege and search for water. When they failed to find any water, they returned to the fortress with the wineskins on their horses filled with wine. The commemoration consists of decoratively harnessed horses galloping up the steep slopes to the Castle.

ⓘ Tourist Office – Calle Monjas, 17
☎   968 702424
www.caravaca.org – click on the link which says callejero for a map.

Ayuntamiento – Plaza Del Arco, 1
☎   968 702000
Bus Station on Carretera de Granada and every hour you can get a bus to Murcia (takes 1 hour and 30 minutes). Daily buses also run to Lorca.
Taxis – ranks on Calle Incomienda and at the corner of Gran Vía and Juan Carlos I
☎   968 708285

Where To Stay
Hotel Central ★ ★ ★
Gran Vía, 18
Luxury hotel – 47 – €65 per night
☎   968 707055

Pensión Victoria ★ ★
Calle María Girón, 1
Central but basic – €39 per night
☎   968 708624

Pensión Patio Andaluz
Gran Vía, 28
€40 per night
☎   968 707682

La Casa de César
Paraje el Bañuelo, 273
Slightly out of town casa rural
☎   968 703 060

Where To Eat

Generally the best food around here is Migas and Tocino de Cielo – a pudding made with egg yolk and syrup. For tapas visit Plaza Del Arco (Mata and Góndola) and Plaza Nueva (Pajaritos, Molowny and El Bodegón).

- Casablanca – Paraje Casablanca – Typical dishes of the region including rice.
- Contamos Contigo – Calle Dos de Mayo, 8 – Cold and hot tapas.
- El Arco – Plaza del Arco, 5 – Meat and fish a speciality.
- El Burladero – Calle Severo Ochoa, 18 – Meat and bulls tail.
- El Cañota – Avda. Gran Vía, 41 – Homemade stews and baby goat.
- El Cortijo – Ctra. de Murcia, 81 – Fresh fish, red meat on the grill and baby goat. Meals under €15 per person.
- El Malena – Próximo al Poligono Industrial Venta Cavila – Game, fresh fish, and mediteranean food
- El Torreón – Calle Los Viñales, 20.
- El Zorro – Pedanía de Barranda – Traditional cooking on the grill
- La Esperanza – Calle Pizarro, 15 – Calamares, migas and leg of lamb.

- La Granja – Pedanía de Archivel – Horse meat prepared like steak on the grill, with peppers and whiskey or Roquefort.
- La Paz – Calle Simancas, n° 12 – Baby goat with garlic, leg of lamb, fish.
- Fuentes del Marqués – Paraje Fuentes del Marqués. – *www.fuentesdelmarques.com* – Game, rice and fish.
- Los Viñales – Avda. Juan Carlos I, n° 41 – Cream of vegetables, onion soup, fried baby goat with garlic and home made puddings.
- Restaurante–Bar–Cafetería Plaza – Plaza Constitución, 5 – Rice, migas, various tapas.
- Rincón de Paco – Calle Lonja, n° 5 – Large selection of Spanish sausages and various tapas.
- Sierra de Mojantes – Pedanía de Archivel. B° de Sta. Bárbara. – Roast meat, rice, migas.
- Sol – Avda. Juan Carlos I, n° 24 – Cold and hot tapas, octopus, and seafood.

Night Life

There are many bars in La Avenida de Espinosa for example Estudiantes, Pancho and C'Pedro. The dancing clubs are found throughout the length of Calle Trafalgar. Rather more chilled might be the club Yeyo and Pegasus. More clubs can be found in Calle Pedro Martínez such as Blanco y Negro (20's to 30's), Zipi–Zape and Hoyo18.

Cartagena and Surrounds

Population: 185,000

Map Reference: E2 0.98°W, 37.60°N

Situated in the south east of the region, it's the second city of Murcia. It's a maritime town with a history stretching back to Roman times. The main road is Paseo de Alfonso XIII, to the south of which lie most areas of interest, including the city's port (pedestrianised area) and tourist sites.

The majority of tourist attractions have a maritime theme, perhaps the most obvious example being the submarine from 1888, which is installed at the port end of the main pedestrianised shopping area.

There is a naval museum, an under water archaeology museum and (although not open to the public) a large arsenal up on the hill overlooking the city. Near the bullring there's a recently re–discovered Roman amphitheatre.

If you have a car you'll be able to drive to many fortresses, castles, fortifications and battlements, ranging from Roman construction through to abandoned 20th century projects. Cartagena's military importance is charted by numerous installations including huge guns on the hilltops, submarine tunnels straight out of a James Bond film set and 16th century pirate look out towers.

Really good web site about walks in Spain, including several around the Cartegena area in particular: *www.andarines.com*

Price List (2005)	Individual	Reduced
The Punic Wall Experience – a fortress with a mysterious culture.	€3.50	€2.50
The History of Cartagena Experience (Concepcion Castle)	€3.50	€2.50
Augusteum – enjoy the grandeur of the empire	€2.50	€2.00
Decumano – experience a Roman Metropolis	€2.00	€1.00
The Museum of Civil War and Air Raid Shelters – special insight into the Spanish civil war, and experience the sensation of a bombing	€3.50	€2.50
Panoramic Lift	€1.00	€0.80
Fortuna House – see what the homes of Roman patricians were like	€2.50	€2.00
Autopsy Pavillion – was used in the past to teach anatomy and carry out autopsies, you can now enjoy various exhibitions.	€1.50	€1.00
Tourist Bus – takes you to Cartagena's most historic sites	€3.50	€2.50
Tourist Boat – sail through the city port and get a closer look at the castles and fortresses that protected the city.	€5.00	€4.00

Special tourist vouchers can be purchased that give substantial discounts. Reduced prices apply to children under 12, students, retired people, disabled people and the unemployed.

The shopping area stretches along Calle Major. Most major Spanish shops can be found here, including El Corte Inglés and Zara.

Remember to look *up* while shopping to see some beautiful facades, many of which have been reformed and rebuilt.

International nautical week in June and in July the Mar de Músicas festival (*www.lamardemusicas.org*) are two of the most popular fiestas.

ⓘ Tourist Office – Plaza de Bastarreche – open on weekdays except for siestas and in the morning on Saturday.
☎ 968 506483
www.ayto–cartagena.es

Ayuntamiento – Calle Sor FCA. Armendariz, 6
☎ 968 128800
www.cartagena.es

Train Stations – Plaza de México, trains running to Murcia and Plaza de Bastarreche, local trains to Los Nietos on the Mar Menor.
Bus station – Calle Trovero Marín
Taxis
☎968 311323 ☎968 531313 ☎968 558038 ☎968 311515

Where To Stay
Hotel Cartagena ★★
Calle Jara, 32
Centrally located, functional but reasonably priced at €36 per night.
☎ 968 502504

Hostal Cartagena
Calle Jara, 32
☎ 968 502500

Hotel Los Habaneros ★★
Calle San Diego, 60
Quite an elegant place for the price at €39 – €48 per night. Pricey restaurant.
☎ 968 502250

Hotel Peninsula ★
Calle Cuatro Santos, 3
Good value, central only €33 per night.
☎ 968 500033

Hotel Alfonso XIII ★ ★ ★ ★
Paseo de Alfonso XIII, 40
€120 per night
☎ 968 520000

Hotel Husa Cartagonova ★ ★ ★ ★
Calle Marcos Redondo, 3
€120 per night
☎ 968 504200

Hotel Manolo ★ ★ ★
Calle Juan Carlos I, 7
Slightly out of town, between €60 –€70 per night
☎ 968 330060
Pensión Isabelita
Plaza María José Artes, 7
€35 per night
☎ 968 507735

Where To Eat
There are three main tapas areas in Cartagena – Calle Major, La Plaza del Rey and the fishing port towards Santa Lucía. Due to the fishing activity in the region octopus, squid and fish are good bets in the area.

- Bahia – Calle Escorial – Seafood and fish.
- El Barril – Calle Del Aire – A fantastic beer bar with careful decoration, a huge variety of tapas of the highest quality.
- Bar La Paz – Alfonso X El Sabio, 16. A great location for breakfast with good tapas.
- Casa Del Pescador – Subida del Nazareno, in the region of Santa Lucía – tapas and seafood.
- Casa Paco – next to la Plaza de Toros – Very economical.
- Casa Pepe – Calle Ramón y Cajal – Excellent tapas.
- Club Billar Cartagena – Paseo Alfonso XIII, 3 – Great variety of tapas – much–frequented by university students.
- Freiduría Tramontana – Calle Jorge Juan, 12. Delicious fried fish and the best calamares in the whole town.

- Mesón Espadas – Calle Jorge Juan, 16. Possibly the largest variety of tapas in the city. Specialties include meaty skewers, scrambled eggs and plenty of local meat, including horse, ostrich and red deer.
- Mesón Sacromonte – Monte Peñas Blancas, 32. Excellent food including fish, tapas and barbecued meat.
- Monterrey – Glorieta de San Francisco.Variety of tapas at a good price.
- Patrick´s II – Paseo Alfonso XIII. An Irish tapas and beer bar. They have excellent tapas with great variety.
- Taibilla – Calle Mayor. Authentic and typical bar with Cartagena tapas. Albóndigas, pork pieces in tomato, pork loin in tomato salsa, and a large tapas selection.
- Tartana, La – Puertas de Murcia. Huge variety of tapas. It's also a restaurant.
- Tasca Del Tío Andrés, La – Alfonso XIII, 46. The best for seafood and octopus.
- Los Habeneros – San Diego, 60 – Great for romantic occasions.

Night Life
Head for the area of Ciudad Jardín where you'll find clubs such as Amigos and El Quijote. There are also a number of bars along Calle Jorge Juán.

Another area to visit is the district of Los Dolores. Along Calle Príncipe de Asturias you can find some disco / pubs such as Copas, Amedeus, La Calle and Príncipe. Jazz and live music can be found in the Peral district – Zanzíbar, El Duende and Vía Lacteá.

The Surrounding Area
There are a number of towns that are in the area of Cartagena, the whole valley is referred to as Campo de Cartagena, which is a huge plain running some 50 km north–south and 50km east–west.

Interesting Places to Visit
La Unión – which has a mining museum (☎968 541792), on Plaza Asensio Sáez – driving around the Cartagena region you won't fail to notice the disused mine works dominating the region.

Los Martínez del Puerto – the only reason to come here, and it's a very good reason, is to visit the Hosteria Rural Las Frailas, on Avenida Juan Carlos I, 26, (☎968 383295). They have an excellent traditional Spanish menu, with an extensive wine list and wonderful and attentive service. Dani, Manolo and Maribel will offer a warm welcome and great suggestions from the day's menu. It's also an excellent place to stay when visiting.

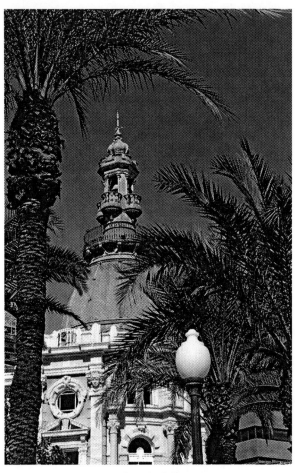

Ayuntamiento in Cartagena

Cehegín

Population: 14,500

Map Reference: C4 1.79°W, 38.09°N

Going due west of Murcia, just before you reach Caravaca and Moratalla, you'll reach the hilltop town of Cehegín. As with several of its neighbours, Cehegín is a medieval town comprising narrow streets and sand coloured buildings. The town is crowned by the Ermita Purísima Concepción, a 16th century creation. From here you get good views of the town and out towards the valley of the river Argos.

There are two fiestas in Cehegín (apart form the usual Easter celebrations) the first being the Muestra de Comercio de Artesanía which is at the end of August. And in September the main town fiesta of La Virgen de Las Maravillas is between the 8th and 14th.

ⓘ Turismo – Calle Begastri, 5
☎   968 723550

Ayuntamiento Calle Lopez Chicheri, 5
☎   968 740400
www.cehegin.com

Where To Stay
Hotel Arcos ★
Ctra Caravaca to Calasparra, km 10
Basic accommodation at €30 per night
☎   968 720707

There are a lot of casa rurales (rural houses for rent) including Paraje Burete, La Estación, Doña Teresa, Los Rosendos, Doña Valentina, Nueva, Tío Naranjas and Tía María. For more information on these get in touch with Noratur ☎ 902 106600.

Hospedería Rural Molino de Sahajosa
Ctra. Cehegín de Calasparra
Rural tourism, but with large rooms and a swimming pool. A double room is €36 per night including breakfast. ☎ 968 720170

Night Life

The nightlife is rather more relaxed with more of a café society feel, you could try Ibiza on Calle Convento or El Molino on Calle Braille. Those with more energy might want to try the disco Sólido which is in Plaza de las Fuerzas Armadas.

Where to Eat

With its clearly inland location Cehegín is a good place for game and lamb. It's also a great place for trying out some of the local wines from the Bullas DOC, in fact there are a couple of Bodegas (wineries) in town: Bodegas Carreño in Calle Jinés de Paco y Gea, 22 and A. Garcia Noguerola, Ctra de Murcia, 102.

- La Almazara – Calle Los Naranjos, 46 – Roast joints of meat, rices and other regional dishes, under €15 per head.
- La Cocina del Convento – Calle Convento, 46 – Good, substantial home made food for under €15 per head.
- El Sol – Calle Major, 17 – Offers nice views over the town, under €15 per person.

Costa Cálida

Map Reference: C1–F2

With 250km of coastline, the Costa Cálida (Warm Coast) is one of Spain's little known holiday hotspots. Along with the Mar Menor the coast of the Costa Cálida is home to water sports, fishing, scuba diving, sun bathing and nature reserves.

The Costa Cálida covers the area from the top of the Mar Menor right along to Águilas. Though the Mar Menor attracts the most visitors, the whole coast has lots to offer. West of Cartagena on the Golfo de Mazarrón the coast is very quiet with many unspoilt beaches and few high rise developments. See Puerto Mazarrón, Bolnuevo and Águilas for a few highlights.

Public transport to these less built up coasts is limited, you'll need your own wheels.

Fortuna

Population: 6,300

Map Reference: E4 1.13°W, 38.18°N

The town is dominated by the spa (Balneario), Roman ruins, the crypt reached through a 200metre tunnel at Manantial Church, a small palace (Palacio Atalaya) and casino. It's also just 2km from the centre the Black Caves (Cueva Negra).

Leana Balneario

3kms outside the town of Fortuna on the Yecla–Pinoso Road is the Balneario, one of only a few hot springs in the Murcia region, just (22km) to the North East of Murcia city. The water quality is amongst the best in Europe for easing rheumatism and arthritis, originally used by the Arabs and the Romans. The spring has waters deep underground, surfacing at temperatures of 53°C, transported straight to the treatment rooms.

The thermal pools are open all day between 10am and 9pm, treatments are available throughout the day. The 3 hotels on site cater for the more expensive end of the market and they are suitably grand. The Balneario even has it's own range of cosmetics and health treatments, which you can buy onsite or through their website: *www.leana.es* (☎902 444410)

Ayuntamiento – Calle Purísima, 7
☎   968 685103

Where To Stay

Hotel Balneario ★ ★ ★
Balneario De Fortuna 30620 – Los Baños
58 rooms
☎   968 685011

Hotel Victoria ★ ★ ★
Balneario De Fortuna 30620 – Los Baños
☎   968 685011

Hotel Costas ★ ★
Ctra. De Abanilla 30620
16 rooms
☎   968 686493

Hotel España ★★
Balneario De Fortuna 30620 – Los Baños
☎ 968 685011

Hotel Los Periquitos ★★
Ctra. De Fortuna, Km 9 30620 – Rambla Salada
☎ 968 685240
www.hotellosperiquitos.com

Hotel La Fuente ★
Camino De La Bocamina 30620 – Los Baños, Small hotel
☎ 968 685125

Fuente Álamo

Population: 10,000

Map Reference: E2 1.17°W, 37.72°N

Going into Fuente Álamo is rather like visiting Croydon. Shut your eyes and listen to the plethora of English accents. We wouldn't like to mislead you into believing that Fuente Álamo is a worthwhile tourist destination, however it does serve a number of useful purposes – including an excellent selection of banks, a Post Office (where you can hire a post office box – Apartado de Correo) and a passable selection of DIY shops.

Fuente Álamo has a new (2005) golf complex to the north west, attracting even more Brits to the area – Hacienda del Álamo.

A good market on a Saturday morning to the north of town (over the bridge) will give you your fix of churros, fruit, veg and dodgy CDs.

Their fiesta, San Agustín, is in August (18th – 28th), when the town resembles a sprawling fun fair.

Ayuntamiento – Plaza Constitucion, 1

www.ayto–fuentealamo.es
☎ 968 597001 or 968 597585

Jumilla

Population: 22,200

Map Reference: D5 1.33°W, 38.48°N

Far off in the north east of the region, as you approach Jumilla you will find the endless acres of vineyards hard to miss! This gives the theme to the whole town, the wine of Jumilla DOC. Overlooking Jumilla is the 15th century castle, which is best seen from the west of the town.

There are many Bodegas and wine shops – there is a strong wine tourist theme. Jumilla is the primary wine–growing region of the whole of Murcia and perhaps the best–known exported wine from the region. Red and rosé wines are particular favourites.

The local fiesta, Vendimia, has a strong wine theme too (what a surprise!) where the catch phrase is "Bebes o Te Mojo" – literally translated as "drink or I'll soak you". The wine flows abundantly so pack some Aspirin!

ⓘ Tourist Office – Avda. de Levante, 13
☎ 968 757682 or 968 716060

Ayuntamiento – Calle Canovas Del Castillo, 35
☎ 968 780112
www.jumilla.org

Buses – Avda. de la Libertad
☎ 968 756242

Taxis – Plaza de la Glorieta
☎ 968 780654

Where To Stay
Hotel Monreal ★ ★ ★
Calle Doctor Fleming, 6
All mod cons, TV, A/C, €54 per night for a double room
☎ 968 781816

> Many towns have a street named after Dr Fleming and there is a statue of him outside the Las Ventas bullring in Madrid. His discovery has saved many lives in Spain but especially those of the bullfighters.

Pensión Pipa ★
Calle Cánovas del Castillo, 150
€27 per night
☎ 968 780124

Night Life
To start the evening you can try having your first drink at Sarao Café, Lady's or Chaplin. Later on you could try Ciudadela, Calimaro, Sinfin (for the younger set) and finally if you fancy Merengue and Salsa till 5 in the morning try Jade Latino.

Where To Eat
There are quite a few tapas opportunities towards the centre of town such as Sotas, Calle Cánovas de Castillo, 56, Nuestro Bar on Calle Milanos, Pueblo Nuevo, La Lonja and Venecia, Calle Doctor Fleming. Gazpacho is a common staple of the town.

Casa Sebastien – Avenida de Levante – this restaurant in the main market is known for its high quality local specialities, where you can eat for less than €15.

- Charco On Tour – Calle Barón del Solar, 66 – less than €15.
- San Agustín – Avenida de la Asunción, 64 – a fish restaurant for less than €15 per person.
- Campo Nuevo – Ctra. De Murcia, Km.
- London – Avda. Levante
- Los Badenes – Ctra. Jumilla–Yecla, Km. 79
- Media Luna – Ctra. Yecla, Km. 75 (La Alquería)
- Meson De Maria – Ctra. Murcia, Km. 58
- Monasterio – Avda. Asunción, 40
- Reyes Catolicos – Avda. Reyes Católicos, 33
- Hnos. Carrion – Fuente Del Pino, 81
- Fuente Del Pino – Fuente Del Pino
- Gran Muralla – Pza. Rey Don Pedro I, 9
- Venta El Rocio – Ctra. De Yecla, Km. 76
- Pueblo Nuevo – La Estacada (Pueblo Nuevo)

Castle in Jumilla

La Manga

Map Reference: F2 0.72°W, 37.66°N

Most Brits who know anything about this region will have heard about La Manga ("the sleeve"), due to its enormous golf course and "housing estate" of the same name and the infamy of British footballers. However La Manga club is somewhat a misnomer as it's actually south of the true La Manga.

The true La Manga is the geographical feature that separates the Mar Menor from the Mediterranean. This heavily developed strip, which is some 21km long and in places only 100m wide, can be seen for tens of kilometres inland. La Manga has a number of pleasant beaches and is in places home to the jet set with a few stunning marinas.

The hotels along La Manga are popular with Spaniards and this really was the first area of tourist development in the region. It's now overrun with Brits and Germans.

La Manga can only be reached by car from the south (Cartagena end) and the spine of La Manga is a busy service road providing access to the hundreds of hotels and holiday flats. Some of the designs would be equally at home in the tasteful (yeah right!) American city of Las Vegas, employing Sandcastles and Boats for their architectural inspiration.

You may walk from La Manga out to the island Isla del Ciervo, where you can get some reasonable views of the other islands on the Mar Menor.

ⓘ Tourist Office
☎   968 146136
Great website with excellent up to date information on the La Manga complex and surroundings: *www.lamangawind.com*

Where To Stay
Dos Mares
Plaza Bohemia
☎   968 140093

Hyatt ★★★★★
Los Belones
Possibly the most expensive hotel in Murcia
☎   968 331234
www.lamanga.hyatt.com

Sol Galúa ★★★★
Hacienda Dos Mares
☎   968 563200
www.solmelia.com

Villas La Manga ★★★★
Gran Vía, km3
☎   968 1452222
www.villaslamanga.es

Where To Eat
There are lots (literally hundreds) of places to eat along the whole strip of the Mar Menor, on the Med side or on the Mar Menor side.

- Restaurante El Parador – In El Vivero, Los Alemanes beach, front line Mar Menor lake. An old house nicely rebuilt. Palm tree garden, beach club, bar. A friendly and warm place in winter. BBQ. One of La Manga restaurants in fashion and therefore expensive.
- ZM 101 – Front line Mar Menor, in El Vivero, Playa de los Alemanes – offers appetisers, drinks, lunch, dinner.
- Restaurante Isla Cristina, Casa Martín, in Puerto Bello, under "Look and Find" office. Good cuisine, reasonable price. Nice place particularly when there is good weather and the outside terrace is open.
- Restaurante La Cañailla in Babilonia housing estate, front line Mediterranean Sea, exit at the level of Km 1.2 Gran Vía de La Manga – Good tapas, excellent fish and sea food, paella rices, stews.

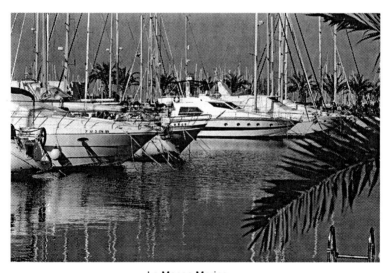

La Manga Marina

Lo Pagán

Population: 1,500

Map Reference: E3 0.79°W, 37.82°N

A seaside toan at the northern most cusp of the Mar Menor, with therapeutic mud baths and a long sandy beach, with calm waters which shelve gently. This is the eastern most town on the Murcian coast, on the tip of the Mar Menor.

The appeal of this area (coupled with San Pedro del Pinatar) revolves around the salt marshes and man–made 'pans' where salt is harvested, now a protected Nature Park. Migrating birds use the marshes as a stop–over and bird–watching is popular. The mineral content of the mud makes it a sought–after remedy or conditioner, especially for the skin, and there are several therapy spas. The towns and beaches themselves combine to form the most popular Mar Menor resort, offering a wide variety of bars and restaurants, plus a good little marina.

On the seafront there is a commercial fish market in the Parque del Mar Juán Carlos I.

Nearby is the regional park of las Salinas, which is home to a variety of protected birds and wild life. On the salt flats you'll find flamingoes and herons in particular, and if you're very lucky a flock will fly overhead while you're bathing on the long sandy beaches.

At the northern end of the town (just as it turns into the one way system, near the windmill – called Molino de Quitín) you can take fantastic walks across the Mar Menor, on a recently renovated path. This path creates a dyke, where on the left handside there are mudbaths and on the right the Mar Menor. If you have the stamina you can walk the length of it (several miles) across to the La Manga side, where you'll find another windmill – called Molino de Calceteras (at Punto de Algas).

The windmill at Punto de Algas is where, if you're lucky, you'll be able to see traditional fishing techniques. You'll also be able to see flamingos on your bracing walk! It's a good spot for a photo.

Where To Stay

Hotel Paloma ★
Calle Río Eresma, 47
With all mod cons including A/C – double from €39 per night.
☎   968 183461

Hotel El Neptuno ★ ★ ★
Avenida del Generalísimo, 19
Plush hotel, open all year, €60
☎   968 181911
www.hotelneptuno.net

Hotel Barceló Lodomar ★ ★ ★ ★
Calle Río Bidasoa, 1
☎   968 186802
www.barcelo.com
Hotel Traiña ★ ★ ★ ★
Avenida del Generalísimo, 84
☎   968 335022
www.hoteltraina.com

Pensión Nieves ★ ★
Calle Andalucía, 1
Aircon and a terrace garden.
☎   968 182040

Where To Eat

Being a seaside town you can expect the ubiquitous fare of pizza and
hamburgers as well as traditional food such as paella and fish.

Salinas Bird Sanctuary

Lorca

Population: 77,500

Map Reference: C2 1.69°W, 37.68°N

Lorca is a genteel city just off the main Águilas – Murcia motorway. The town's most interesting architecture is from the 16th century onwards.

Its castle is prominently visible from far off and Lorca forms another portal to the Sierra Espuña. The castle started out as an Islamic fortress between the 8th and 13th centuries and the oldest parts of the castle, the essential water systems, still remain. Today the castle is used for many town activities including fiestas and civic functions. Entrance costs €12 with lots of local history exhibits to view.

Lorca's Easter celebrations are probably the most splendid in Murcia (depending upon whom you talk to!) The local fiesta is on the 8th September for la Virgen de Las Huertas.

La Casa de Guevara is a Baroque building belonging to the Guevara family built between 1689 and 1705. There is a beautiful courtyard and wonderful period interior rooms, including a great collection of paintings. ☎902 400047 for opening hours and rates.

Possibly the most outstanding church in Lorca is La Colegiata de San Patricio, which was built between the 16th and 18th centuries and towers over the central part of town. The Iglesia de San Mateo which was built principally in the 18th and 19th century has a stunning vaulted interior.

The town has a number of museums including the Museo de Arqueológico Municipal, which is on Plaza de Juan Moreno (968 406267), open Tuesday to Saturday (closed for siesta) and Sunday mornings. There is also an embroidery museum.

The Ayuntamiento (17th and 18th century) is actually worth a look inside since it contains enormous canvasses depicting past battles around Lorca. It also has a collection of contemporary paintings by local artists.

One central landmark is the Columna Milenaria which is a Roman milepost from 10 BC from the time of emperor Augustus on which a sculpture of San Vincente was placed in the 15th century.

Continuing west from Lorca you reach the town of Puerto Lumbreras, the final town in Murcia. Not too much to say about this town, except that at the moment it has the region's only Parador (which really isn't worth the money). However this will soon change when the new Parador in Lorca (on the site of the Moorish castle) is opened.

If you want to stay over at this Western most corner of Murcia, where it meets Almería, then Cortijo de la Noria could be just what you're looking for. Run by a British couple, they offer everything from quads, 4x4, horseriding and a large swimming pool: *www.cordelano.com*

ⓘ Tourist Office – Calle Lope Guisbert, 12 – open weekdays apart from siestas and in Summer it opens in the afternoons during the weekends. There are good guides in English available.
☎ 968 466157
www.ajuntalorca.es

Ayuntamiento – Plaza De España
☎ 968 407000

Trains – on the Murcia – Águilas line, on the outskirts of town towards the motorway junction.

Bus Station – next to the train station, not only to Murcia but also Granada (3 times per day)

Taxis – ranks at Plaza de Calderón, Plaza Ortega Melgares, Calle Glorieta de San Vicente and Plaza Óvalo. You can call a cab on ☎968 471110.

Where To Stay
Hotel Alameda
Musso Valiente
Central, with all mod cons, 45 – 58 Euros per night.
☎ 968 406600

Hotel Amaltea ★ ★ ★ ★
Ctra de Granada
84 –114 Euros per night
On the outskirts of town with large gardens, three lakes joined by
small cascades and an impressive pool with a Jacuzzi.
☎ 968 406565
www.nh–hotels.com

Jardines de Lorca ★ ★ ★ ★
Alameda Rafael Méndez
79 – 91 Euros per night
☎ 968 470599
www.hotelesdemurcia.com

Hotel Félix ★
Avenida de las Fuerzas Armadas, 14
Recently renovated with rooms at 33 – 35 Euros per night, all rooms
have aircon, tv and their own bathroom.
☎ 968 467654

Hostal el Carmen ★ ★
Rincón de los Valientes, 3
€35 per night
☎ 968 466459

Pensión Casa Juan ★ ★
Calle Guerra, 10
€36 per night, central
☎ 968 468006

Pensión La Alberca ★ ★
Plaza Juan Moreno, 1
☎ 968 406516

Night Life

Starting in the Plaza de España, you can begin with tapas in Bacco and La Caña, move onto Calle del Alamo where you can go to Acquario with live jazz and Fraguel Rock which also has live music. Jazz can also be found at Pasaje 30 on Calle Corredera. You could then try Zero and several bars along Avenida de Juan Carlos I.

Discos going on late into the night are Silos and Joker.

Where To Eat

- Casa Roberto – Calle Musso Valiente, 5 – Modern restaurant with reasonable priced fixed menu.

- Rincón de los Valientes – Rincón de los Valientes, 13 – Traditional, local food at a good price at the west end of town.

- Jardines de Lorca – Alameda Rafael Méndez

- Casa Cándido – Calle Santo Domingo, 13 – Offering traditional Murcian food including shrimps and stuffed calamares. Nice dungeons – ask for a tour!

- El Teatro – Plaza de Colón, 12 – A mixture of new and old Spanish cooking, upmarket!

- Juan de Toledo – Juan de Toledo, 14 – Offers a reasonable price set menu, close to the centre of town.

Los Alcázares

Population: 6,000

Map Reference: E2 0.85°W, 37.74°N

Central on the west side of the Mar Menor, its name comes from the Arab Al–kazar. The Romans and then later the Arabs used this town as an ideal location for thermal baths. You can still enjoy the benefits of the spas in the hotel La Encarnación.

In August (15th – 30th) they have their local fiesta – Semana de la Huerta – when groups representing market garden areas throughout Spain and other European countries gather to display their folklore, handicrafts and prepare gastronomic feasts from their local produce. Fiestas are popular here; there's a week–long fiesta in mid October and a Medieval one at the end of March.

From the port you can get excursions to the Isla Perdiguera which is inside the Mar Menor. On the island there's a restaurant where you can get grilled sardines. Build up your appetite with some excellent swimming.

In 2005 all 5 local beaches were awarded the highest grade possible for water quality and have EEC Blue Flag status. Following an inspection covering facilities, safety, signage and sand quality Playa del Espejo and Playa Manzanares were given Grade A (Optimum) and Playas Las Palmeras, Carrion and La Concha received Grade B (Good). The town was the first in the region to achieve the coveted Q Certification for quality of beaches and the town's Tourist Information facilities have also earned a Q Certificate. This is a tribute to the efforts of the 60 municipal employees who work all year round to keep the beaches in perfect condition.

A commercial bike scheme will be introduced with initially 300 machines available for hire at a modest charge. This will fit in perfectly with the plan to build a network of cycle tracks throughout the town.

A botanical garden covering 40,000 sq meters will be constructed adjacent to Nueva Ribera and the La Hita beach.

Other projects include a new Conference Centre (Palacio de Congresos), Cultural Centre, School of Nautical Activities and Tourist Information Centre.

The newish Balneario Commercial Centre near the Mercadona has over a dozen food outlets including an excellent Thai/Vietnamese/Cantonese (Cocina Asiatica Run) and good Indian (Hindustani Roti Sharaabi Bar). There is also a Kodak photo shop, the Postal Room for internet use and postal service to the UK, various beauty salons and cycle hire. Nearby on the north side of the Avenida de la Libertad is El Patio IV which is a large Spanish restaurante specializing in meat dishes cooked on a huge open grill (veggies beware).

A short distance along the Ave de la Libertad is the Oasis Centre which has a mixture of more eating establishments including some that cater for the all–day breakfast brigade. For those who are home–sick there is the Big Breakfast Butchers which can provide British cuts, barbecue meats and home–made sausages.

Los Alcázares is very Spanish with a maze of narrow interesting streets. Parking seems to be easy apart from July–August when the Spanish arrive on holiday.

ⓘ Tourist Office – Calle Fuster, n° 63
☎ 968 171361
www.losalcazares.com

Where To Stay
There are some campsites locally, Alcázeres ☎968 575100

Hotel Corzo ★ ★ ★
Calle La Base, 6
☎ 968 575125
www.hotelcorzo.com

Hotel Cristina ★ ★ ★
Calle La Base, 2
☎ 968 171110
www.cristinahotel.net

Hotel Pagán ★ ★ ★
Avenida Constitución (los Narejos)
☎ 968 575 080
www.hotelpagan.com

Where To Eat
There are lots of places to eat including plenty of pizza restaurants and British run bars.

Mar Menor
Map Reference: E2–F2

This is a closed sea which maintains a warm sea temperature in whatever stage of the year (except December and January when only the most hardy Brits will brave the waters!) – with an average of 18 degrees centigrade. The Romans and the Arabs built thermal baths around the coast, and to this day people visit the area for the therapeutic properties of the bathing.

It has 170km^2 of area (42,000 acres) and 73 km of coast. The Mar Menor is the largest salt lagoon in Europe. Its waters are rich in iodine and never get deeper than 7 metres.

There are considerable salt works in the area which coincide with important ecological reserves for birds, plants and other wildlife.

Langoustines are another delicacy pulled out of the Mar Menor (along with the caviar).

To get a good view of the Mar Menor, take a walk up the hill Cabezo de la Fuente from Los Belones village (near La Manga golf complex)

Some notable beaches (also see Los Alcázares, San Pedro del Pinatar, Lo Pagán, Santiago de la Ribera) include:

Los Urrutias – A relatively new resort, Los Urrutias has almost a mile of golden beach with good facilities, enhanced by an unusual offshore marina in a hexagonal shape. Behind the beach is a modern, spaciously laid out town with an attractive promenade and public spaces. The coast either side is protected land, preserving the quality of the environment.

Los Nietos – Divided into an 'old town' just off the coast and a newer resort area with a very good beach, Los Nietos is another Mar Menor town with a popular marina. A great place to eat in Los Nietos is Pescador Ros only open in summer months, a bit scruffy looking, but good food and not too expensive. Big enough to have a life all year round, it is popular with buyers seeking a place to live, as well as holidaymakers. Linked to the city of Cartagena by rail, it is especially suitable for those who prefer to travel by public transport.

Mar de Cristal – Separated from Los Nietos by a small river, Mar de Cristal is a compact and friendly little resort with three good beach areas and a new, pretty promenade with bars and restaurants. A good sized marina adds to the charm.

Playa Honda & Playa Paraiso – At the very southern end of the Mar Menor, these two beach areas have seen quite a bit of expansion in the last few years and have evolved into fully–fledged resorts. It is nestled with the hills of the Calablanque Nature Park behind, the protected Marchamalo salt flats to the side and the whole length of the Mar Menor in front.

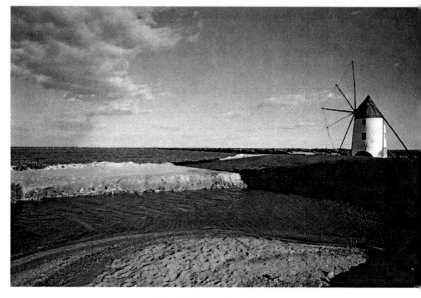

Windmill at the Mar Menor

Mazarrón

Population: 20,900

Map Reference: D2 1.31°W, 37.60°N

A functional market town that has sprung up out of the old mining industry in the area. The region used to mine the mountain ranges which were rich in lead, zinc, silver, iron and alum. The remnants of the mining industry can be seen throughout the region.

This is the central shopping area for a number of satellite housing estates, such as Camposol.

There are many useful DIY (bricolage) shops just out of town towards Puerto Mazarrón and the outskirts.

ⓘ Tourist Office – Avenida Doctor Meca, 47
☎   968 594426

The ayuntamiento on Plaza de Ayuntamiento (strangely!)
☎   968 590119
www.mazarron.es

Taxis

☎   968 590676 Calle Juan Paredes
☎   968 595122 – Plaza del Muelle
☎   968 594715 for outlying areas

Bus Station – Avenida Doctor Meca – there are 3 buses per day to nearby Cartagena.

Where to Stay
Pensión Calventus II
Avenida de la Constitucion, 60
☎   968 590094

Guillermo II ★★
Calle Carmen, 7
Between €31 and €42 per night
☎   968 590436
www.mazarron.com/holidays/guillermo
www.hotelguillermo2.com

Moratalla

Population: 9,000

Map Reference: B4 1.89°W, 38.19°N

Moratalla is an old town of Arab origin with narrow streets, rambling up a steep hillside, off to the northwest of the province.

The town is capped by a castle with excellent views to the surrounding countryside and forest. It makes a good base for walking and cycling.

In the centre of town on Calle Constitución there's a 16th – 18th century convent, Convento de San Francisco, with an exhibit room.

The fiesta for Moratalla is between the 11th and 17th of July for Cristo del Rayo.

ⓘ   Tourist Office
www.moratalla–turismo.com

Ayuntamiento – Calle de la Constitución
☎   968 730258
Bus Station – ctra de Caravaca – daily buses to Caravaca de la Cruz.
☎   968 292211
Taxis
☎   968 730653 and 968 730430

Places To Stay
Camping at La Puerta, out of the town at the village of La Puerta, 7km up the valley to the north west – ☎968 730008. It has a restaurant and swimming pool.

There are a couple of rural tourism possibilities run buy NORATUR ☎902 106600. For example there is Hospedería Rural la Tejera on the road to La Puerta at kilometer 2.

Hospedería Rural Molino de Benizar ☎968 706600.

Hotel Cenajo ★ ★ ★
Pantano de Cenajo
Out of town, so you'll need a car. Between 67–93 Euros per night.
☎   968 721011

Pensión Reyes ★
Calle Tomás el Cura, 7
A basic pension in the middle of town. €24 per night.
☎   968 730377

Night Life
Night life mainly happens in the summer, out on the Ctra. de Caravaca where there are a number of café pubs. At weekends you can also find a lot of more lively entertainment along Ctra. de Campo de San Juan.

Where To Eat
For tapas walk along Calle Major to find various bars to choose from.

- Reyes – Calle Tomás el Cura, 7
- Bar Luquillas – Ctra. San Juan, 34 – Good for tapas.

Mula

Population: 14,600

Map Reference: D3 1.49°W, 38.04°N

Mula is on the river Mula, and is another hillside town topped with a castle (like Moratalla). Many of the streets appear to be pedestrianised and you'll be surprised to find a car in the most unlikely of places! Mula is also the epicentre for a geological faultline, and has experienced a number of minor earthquakes – in 1999, 2002 and most recently in 2005.

At the centre of town you'll find the small park of La Glorieta Juan Carlos I, and around the park is the convent and church of San Francisco. The town also has a museum, Museo de el Cigarralejo, open Tuesdays to Sundays in the mornings.

There are a number of churches around town including Iglesia de San Miguel (16th century), Iglesia de Carmen (18th century) and Iglesia de Santo Domingo (16th century).

Castillo de los Vélez (the castle on top of the hill) is 16th century and can be reached by footpaths which meander up from the top of town.

Local fiestas between the 19th and 25th of September (el Niño de Mula) and also the 15th May for the fiesta of San Isidoro. The Easter celebrations are particularly vibrant in Mula due to the drumming!

ⓘ Tourist Office – Calle Doña Elvira
☎ 968 661501
www.mulavirtual.net (good street map and an A–Z – click on "Callejero")

Ayuntamiento – Plaza Del Ayuntamiento
☎ 968 660444
Bus Station – Senda de la Moreira – has buses to Murcia and Caravaca
☎ 968 292211

Where To Stay

Hospedería Rural Casas Nuevas – can sleep upto 24 people for around €48 per 2 people per night. Excellent for walking in the Sierra Espuña.
☎ 902 106600

Hospedería Rural Molino de Filipe – out of town in the Rivera de los Molinos, 321.
☎ 902 106600

Call Noratur on ☎902 106600 for many more Casas Rurales.

Alcázar ★ ★
Ctra de Pliego
☎ 968 662105

Where To Eat

For tapas the best spot is off the park of Glorieta Juan Carlos I where you'll find many places.

There are various places to eat, mostly out of town towards Baños de Mula or Niño de Mula.

- Restaurant Gini – Calle Juan Martínez Soto, 13 – Outdoor terrace, serving typically Spanish food, including rice, meat and bacalao.
- El Churrasco – Calle Fray Pedro Botía, 4 – Specialising in Churrasco and paella.
- Mesón Rural – Calle Ortega y Rubio, 5 – Various tapas and home cooked foods, open every day.

Murcia and Surrounds

Population: 370,800

Map Reference: E3 1.13°W, 37.98°N

The city of Murcia is set in the heart of a rich fertile plain at just 43 metres above sea level. Unlike the rest of the region, where the terrain is dry and rugged, the soil here is irrigated by the River Segura and the land has been widely and fruitfully cultivated.

In the city itself the old quarter is made up of a maze of narrow streets huddled together around the Cathedral. This labyrinth is only broken by the main roads crossing through it such as the Gran Vía Escultor Salzillo.

The most pleasant parts of the city, indeed the most typically Murcian, are to be found around the gardens on the banks of the River Segura. A considerable part of the population of Murcia do not in fact live in the city itself, rather they live in houses and farmsteads scattered around it. A wide variety of fruits and vegetables are grown not only for the Spanish domestic market but also for export to the rest of Europe. For this reason Murcia is often referred to as La Huerta de Europa: The Market Garden of Europe.

What is there to do in Murcia City?

A good website to look at before leaving the UK is: *www.murciaciudad.com*

Sadly it's not great for navigating, but it does have an interactive city map, which is very useful.

For a monthly updated guide take a look on (small printed booklets can be picked up for free at the tourist information centres and some bars): *www.laguiago.com*

Murcia is an ancient, Mediterranean, and hospitable city which was founded and fortified in 825 AD by Abderraman II with the name Mursiya in the fertile planes of the Segura.

Murcia, paradise of light and the orange blossom, is a happy and extroverted city, highlighted by: the Cathedral – Catedral de Santa María, the Church of Our Father Jesus (home to the museum of the celebrated sculptor Salzillo), the Episcopal Palace, the Convent of Santa Ana, the Church of San Miguel, the Monastery of Santa Clara la Real, El Almudi, the Sancutary of Fuensanta, the Gardens of Malecón, and the Casino.

PLAZA CARDINAL BELLUGA

Nothing could be more relaxing than making the short drive into the city on a Sunday morning, and sitting in the Plaza Cardinal Belluga with your newspaper (La Verdad for Marcus and El Semanal for me – I like the pictures!) and a coffee and tostadas, watching the world go by. On many occasions we've been entertained by marching bands, balloon sellers or by watching cars magically appear out of buildings.

The Casino is €1.20 to get in and is on Calle Trapería, 22. It's certainly worth a special visit for the fantastic stained glass and Arabic tiles, combined with colonial feel and good coffee. Additionally for members there is a library, meeting rooms, a billiard room and a ballroom.

The Cathedral was built between the 14th and 18th centuries, with some parts being rebuilt in 1735 after flood damage. You can get great views, almost 100 metres up, in the tower which dates from the 18th century.

Across from the Cathedral is a striking modern building which is part of the Ayuntamiento complex, which surprisingly complements the Baroque cathedral facing it across the square at Plaza Cardenal Belluga. This building was designed by Rafael Moneo.

The Jardin Floridablanca is a great place to escape the heat of summer under the shade of its well–established rubber trees. It was established in 1848 by Carlos III and was the first public garden to be built in Spain.

Other points of interest are the Museum of Murcia and the Hydraulic Museum, the water mills of the Segura river in Murcia and the surrounding villages which make up the Region.

Murcia also benefits from a diverse programme of festivities: carnivals (February), Easter (March/April), the Spring Festivals (March/April), the Fair of Murcia (September), and Christmas (December), which, together with cinema, theatre, and music festivals, conferences, and art exhibitions mark out the animated cultural life in the city. Many of these events take place in the "Teatro Romea" and "Centro de Congresos" of the Region of Murcia.

Easter is a perfect time to visit Murcia to see a traditional Spanish fiesta – Semana Santa – the ornate wooden sculptures of the city's famous artist, Salzillo, are paraded throughout the city. Just after Semana Santa, the Spring Festival (*Fiestas de Primavera*) is a week–long party that includes the outstanding Bando de la Hurta and the *Entierro de la Sardina* ('burying of the sardine').

BANDO DE LA HUERTA

On the first Tuesday after Easter this one day in particular stands out – Bando De La Huerta ('proclamation of the countryside'). If there's one fiesta that you should go to all year in Murcia (apart from your local village's, of course), this is it. Simply eschewing shorts and tee shirts will not be enough to prevent you from standing out as the *extranjero* in this fiesta. About 90% of the people at the festival wear national dress, so take a camera! There are lots of stalls (*barracas*) where you might be lucky to get a sample of traditional local food and drink – alternatively, all the restaurants and bars will be open. The processions and entertainment start in mid afternoon and go on all night – have a good siesta beforehand and enjoy!

Practicalities: You'll need to get hold of some national dress (lots of adverts for places selling it in the local Murcia press during the weeks leading up to the festival). Try and get a copy of the local newspaper (e.g. *La Verdad*) on the Monday before to get the running schedule for the day. We parked out on the East side of town (near the river) and walked the couple of kilometers into town – you don't want to even *try* to get closer than this with your car. Also be very careful when leaving by car – you may be under the limit, but not many others will be! If you drive in about 3pm, you'll find that the roads coming into town are eerily deserted – everybody's getting some rest before the real partying.

Hospital – The region's main hospital is to the south west of the city off the Murcia to Caravaca highway, called Arixicaca, between el Palmar and Alcantarilla.

Shopping
El Cortes Inglés – Avenida de la Libertad

There are lots of shops along Gran Vía and its side streets. Also in the streets between Calle el Escultor Salzillo to the west and Calle Saavedra Fajardo. Excellent shoe and clothes shopping as you'd expect in a main modern Spanish city.

Books – Diego Marín, Merced, 9–11 – selling lots of local maps and the Natursport guides (you just need to find them – there appears to be no logic in the shop's layout!). ☎968 242296, *www.diegomarin.com*

Maps – La Casa del Mapa, Palacio de las Balsas, Plaza Balzas, 1. Upstairs on the first floor of this local government building, you'll enter a mapping paradise, as long as your world revolves around Spain. The map stocks are exhaustive, including all the 1:25,000 topographical / military maps. The only problem with this shop is the opening hours – 9 – 14:00 Monday to Friday, only. ☎968 21 01 96, *www.cnig.es*

There is a crafts centre at el Centro de Artesania on Calle Francisco Rabal, 8. Excellent furniture and homeware shops at interesting prices surround these narrow streets.

On Barrio del Carmen (near Floridablanca) you can find Armaría Del Carmen (with another outlet in Cartagena near the train station) which sells guns, fishing tackle and scuba gear. There are lots of other good shops in this area too, and it's a great place for a bit of people watching on a Saturday morning.

Outside the city there are Carrefour and Eroski to the east on the ring road, with another branch of Carrefour to the north and a Makro to the southwest.

There's a large Polígono, good for furniture and building materials to the south west, just off the main road to Caravaca.

Buying cameras and other photo equipment in Murcia isn't cheap compared to on–line places elsewhere in Europe, although at least you will be able to take it back when it goes wrong. Try El Corte Inglés in Murcia for a good selection.

If you are stuck in the 20th century (like us) and still need to get films developed, there are some high street places in Murcia that will develop and print a 36 exposure 35mm on a 1 day turnaround for about €8, for example Fotoprix on Calle Saavedra Fajardo 4 in Murcia. For top notch film processing and services (printing, reversal prints, etc.) you can go to Murcia Color, Avenida El Descubrimiento S/N, Poligono Industrial Oeste, Murcia (*www.murciacolor.com*) – beware, they aren't cheap, but for wedding photos, etc. they're probably the best in Murcia.

In February 2006 Ikea opened a new store just on the outskirts of Murcia, exit 763A on the A7 road to Alicante, just north of Murcia city. It's a big one! Check for opening times on their website *www.ikea.com*

For a huge selection of household electrical, computers, software, DVDs and music you could visit MediaMarkt, Ronda Sur Zona Infante. Or for more specialist electronics and electrical bits and pieces (like power supplies for a wireless router) try Electronica RAYTE right opposite the RENFE train station (which is good for parking for Barrio del Carmen and Floridablanca!) at Plaza Industria.

The Fuensanta and El Valle Natural Park

The patron saint of Murcia is La Virgen de la Fuensanta. A shrine is dedicated to her, 6 km to the south of the city. From here visitors can enjoy splendid views over the Huerta. Continuing on, you arrive at El Valle Natural Park, areas of which have an almost lunar like appearance. The park is of great geological importance.

From the panoramic view point, the "Cresta del Gallo" (The Cock's Crest), which is set at the foot of the peak from which it gets its name, one can enjoy impressive scenery. Continuing along the road you arrive at another vantage viewpoint "Columbares" which is south facing. The total distance of the excursion is approximately 32 km.

ⓘ Tourist Office – the main turismo is at Plaza de Julián Romea, 4 (opposite the theatre) – open weekdays except during the siesta
☎ 902 101070
There is another at Plaza Cardenal Belluga.
There is also a kiosk at Plaza San Francisco ☎968 216801
www.murciaciudad.com or *www.murciaturistica.es*
Ayuntamiento – Glorieta de España, 1
☎ 968 358600
www.ayto–murcia.es

The main bus station is to the west of centre on Calle Sierra de la Pila, 1
☎ 968 292211
Taxis are by the train and bus stations and at various other places around the city such as Plaza Martinez Tornel, Avenida de la Libertaz and Calle Alfonso X. You can also call for a taxi on
☎968 248800 or ☎968 297700.

Train Station – Plaza de la Industria, to the south of town
☎ 968 252154

Where To Stay
Pensíon Hispano I ★★
Calle La Trapería, 8
Very central, near the Cathedral, €36 per night
☎ 968 216152
www.hotelhispano.net

Hotel Hispano II
Calle Radio Murcia, 3
☎ 968 216152
www.hotelhispano.net

Hotel Rincón de Pepé ★★★★
Calle Apóstoles, 34
Upmarket, from 57 to 168 Euros per night
☎ 968 212239
www.nh–hotels.com

Hotel Amistad Murcia ★★★★
Condestable, 1
Upmarket, from 57 to 238 Euros per night, near El Corte Ingles
☎ 968 282929
www.nh–hotels.com

Pensíon Avenida
Calle Canalejas, 10
Just on the southside of the river.

☎   968 215294

Pensíon Segura ★★
Plaza de Camachos, 19
€30 per night
☎   968 211281

Where To Eat

In Murcia, there are a great number of bars and squares where you can enjoy a delicious appetiser in the open air. The most well–known Murcian tapas include: pisto, zarangollo and la ensalada murciana, all of which are prepared with vegetables from the rich Murcian markets. Some of the most popular bars are El Palomo and Los Toneles, both situated in Calle Cánovas del Castillo, the Pepico del Tío Ginés in Calle las Mulas, Los Zagales in Calle Polo de Medina, El Patio in Calle Paco and La Parranda situated in Plaza San Juan.

At weekends, the bars serving tapas in Plaza del las Flores, la Plaza Mayor, and Alfonso X el Sabio are much frequented. If you want a formal meal, there are restaurants in every part of the city where you can find great quality at a fair price.

GREAT FOOD & GREAT WINE!

Just outside of the city, in El Palmar there is an excellent restaurant, which has a superb wine cellar (not that that influenced our opinion – well not until the second bottle of superb wine!). Try them out at Casa Bernal – c/ Mayor, 90, 30120–El Palmar–Murcia tel. 68 884304

The form seems to be they bring you beautifully prepared and arranged starters. They don't stop until you look ready to burst, then they ask what you might like to try for your second course! Their steaks are superb.

Please save space for a homemade dessert, or try their wonderful selection of cheeses.

And did we mention their wine? Ask for their recommendation by the glass with each course (or with each starter if you're not driving!)

A great site at *www.atapear.com* is devoted to tapas all over Spain.

In Murcia city, the best tapas can be found around Plaza de las Flores and Arco de San Juan.

Cafés are centred along Gran Vía Alfonso X and Plaza de Santa Domingo.

- Arco – Arco de Santo Domingo, 1 – Lots of good specialities, try anchovies with pimientos and potatos.
- Casino – Calle de la Trapería – 3 course set menu.
- Continental – Barítono Marcos Redondo, 6 – Great tapas.
- Corral de Jose Luis, El– Plaza de Santo Domingo, 23. The queen of vegetarian tapas.
- Churra, El – Marqués de los Vélez, 12. Roast potatoes with garlic, Zarangollos (see above) and great puddings.
- Fénix – Plza de Santa Catalina, 1 – Octopus cooked in the oven and caballitos (not the literal translation of little horses, but prawn tails).
- Hispano II – Calle Arquitecto Cerdán – really good set menus.
- Mesón de Pepe – Calle Arquitecto Emilio Pérez Piñero. Oven cooked lamb.
- Paco Pepe – Madre de Dios, 14. One of the best restaurants in Murcia.
- La Parranda – Plaza de San Juán – Typical Murcian tapas. Local cheese, potatoes with garlic mayonnaise and salads.
- Pepe el Torrao – Ronda Norte, 6. Caballitos (prawn tails), octopus, shellfish gallician style, red prawns from Santa Pola.
- Perela, El – Calle Ruiperez, 5 – Great tapas in a good atmosphere.
- Perico del Tío Ginés – Calle Ruipérez, 4 – Good wine from Jumilla to go with your "blayeres", which are rolls stuffed with "other things".
- Rincón de Pepe – Apóstoles, 34. Excellent quality tapas, including mojama (cured tuna) and other local specialities. Widely reported to be one of the best restaurants in Murcia.
- Taberna de las Mulas – Calle Ruipérez, 7 – Specialising in goat dishes.
- Tapa, La – Plaza de las Flores, 13 – Great variety of tortillas and an impressive quantity of tapas.

- Toneles, Los – Canovas del Castillo, 7 – Mainly vegetarian options, with local produce.

Veggie restaurants in Murcia

- El Girasol, C/ San José, 22 – ☎ 968 21 29 65
- Maná, Pza. Junterones, 6 – ☎ 968 28 58 24
  www.vegetarianomana.com

Night Life

Murcia boasts authentic Spanish nightlife centred on the area between Calle Saavedra Fajardo and Museo de Bellas Artes. Late night bars are found around the north end of Gran Vía Alfonso X and its side streets.

The evenings kick off in the bars along Calle Alfaro, as things move on you should look for Calle Enrique Villar Bas for some dicso pubs. Disco bars worth trying are B12 on Calle Trinidade, 17 and El Perro Azul. There's an Irish theme pub where you might hear some English on Plaza Cetina.

You'll find various dance halls along Calle San Lorenzo.

During university terms there are lots of gigs which are listed in the free publications – Sample and Murcia Anderground: *www.murcianderground.com*

Jazz can be found at La Puerta Falsa on Calle San Martin de Porres, 5 and La Muralla del Rincón de Pepe on Calle Cánovas del Castillo.

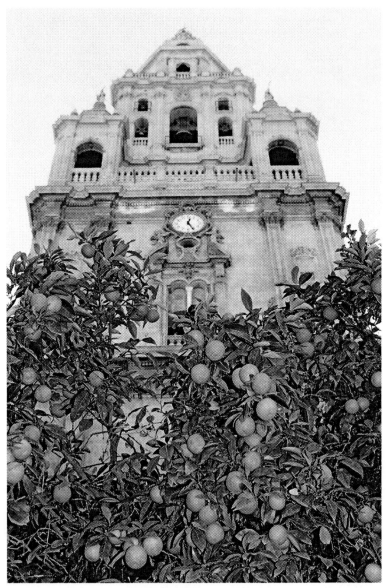

Murcia Cathedral with oranges

Puerto Mazarrón

Population: 5,000

Map Reference: D1 1.26°W, 37.59°N

Not to be confused with Mazarrón, this seaside town is the centre of much of tourism on the south coast and Mediterranean.

There are good beaches as you head out of town (North East) and all along the coast towards Aquilas – in fact 35km of them (just a small part of the 250 km of coastline in the Costa Cálida)!

ⓘ Tourist Office – Calle Doctor Meca, 20
☎ 968 594426

Where To Stay
There are plenty of campsites – for example:
Garoa, Playa de Mazarrón – on the road towards Bolnuevo
☎ 968 150660
Camping Los Delfines – towards La Azohia
☎ 968 594527
Camping Los Madriles – towards La Azohia
☎ 968 152151

There are lots of hotels in this area, here's a selection.

Hostal La Línea ★★
Calle Cartagena, 2
Diego and Encarna run this comfortable (though the rooms are small) hostal, with aircon and bathrooms and some of the best tapas in Murcia.
☎ 968 594549

Pensión Delphín
Caudillo, 13
☎ 968 594639

Hotel Playa Grande ★ ★ ★
Avenida Castellar, 19
Upmarket hotel right on the beach, 45–75 Euros per night. The hotel has the restaurant "La Meseguera" with specialities of typical Murcian Food.
☎ 968 594684
www.hotel–playagrande.com

Where to Eat

Puerto Mazarrón is certainly no centre of gastronomy. Our favourite restaurant from the previous edition of the guide (Virgen del Mar on the seafront) has disappeared under the concrete being used for the harbour area redevelopment.

- Casa del Mar – Paseo de la Sal – on the old fishing harbour. Popular place with rice and fish as specialities (a reasonable alternative to the now defunct Virgen del Mar). Discount for divers coming from Zoea across the road!
- Bel de Mar – Avenida Costa Cálida – part fishmongers and part cafeteria, for good, fresh fish, that you select yourself. Bel de Mar is very close to the Turismo.
- La Línea – Calle Cartagena, 2 – some of the best tapas in Murcia

On the seafront there are many places to buy cheap platos combinados and do a little tourist shopping. Also, there are about a million (OK, a slight exaggeration) Chinese restaurants in Puerto Mazarrón. Our intolerance of MSG prevents us from trying them all, but, statistically, at least one of them must be good.

Night Life

Is centred around Calle Axial where you'll find clubs El Embarcadero, El Palmito and La Casona. And along the seafront you'll find plenty of disco–pubs which are open in the summer.

Ricote Valley
Map Reference = D4 1.35°W, 38.15°N

The Ricote Valley was the last stronghold of the Moors in Spain, and is one of the most beautiful and undiscovered parts of Murcia, along the fertile plains of the river Segura. The region clings to its Arab heritage, as shown by the numerous remains from this period, including the ingenious rural irrigation system.

Ricote maintains a rich and highly individual gastronomic tradition in which the local wine features strongly, how pleasant! After indulging in the delights of the local cuisine, you may feel like enjoying a few days of healthy relaxation and pampering at the wonderful 19th century spa in Archena very close by.

Sporting activities such as river–rafting on the River Segura, mountain biking or horse riding along routes offered by various riding centres are the most popular activities.

The main towns and villages include: Villanueva, Ulea, Ojós, Ricote and Blanca.

Ojos in the Ricote Valley

San Javier

Population: 20,200

Map Reference: E2 0.84°W, 37.85°N

Probably best known as the local name for Murcia airport (2 miles away), since 1998 San Javier has been the home of an increasingly popular jazz festival in late June. San Javier itself is just off the coast, a well–established town with a long history illustrated in its museum. It has excellent shopping and leisure facilities, including an impressive sports centre.

A town just inland from the Mar Menor, its tortuous one way system is probably known to most first time visitors to San Javier airport! However, once on foot you can visit some 17th century churches, including La Ermita and the Iglesia de la Virgen del Rosario.

ⓘ Tourist Office – Calle Padre Juan (Centro Socio Cultural Príncipe de Asturias) in Santiago de la Ribera (close by)
☎ 968 571704
www.turismosanjavier.net – good town maps (click on Callejero)

Ayuntamiento – Glorieta Garcia Alix
☎ 968 571401

The nearest train station is in Balsicas, 10km away.
Buses – Autobus Urbano – Autocares La Inmaculada
☎ 968 180659 or 968 571401 or 968 571047

The Airport

The Murcia–San Javier (MJV) airport is on the coast of the Mar Menor to the south of San Pedro del Pinatar. The airport is supposedly due to be replaced by the fabled new airport between Corvera and Valladolises. However it is steadily expanding from its initial single baggage belt in 2003 to 4 in 2005. It still retains some of its quaint one–horse–town feel and also shares the runway with the local airforce training jets. A parking fee was introduced in 2006, so the days of free longterm airport parking are over!

The airport is primarily military and is home to the Spanish Aeronautical School headed by the King of Spain.

Transport from the airport is restricted to taxis and a journey to the City of Murcia will cost about €60. Many of the travellers coming in to Murcia airport stay on the Costa Cálida and do not visit the city of Murcia. The closest train station is in Balsicas. A taxi all the way into Murcia city costs around €60, or you can get a bus (latbus number 73) direct to the city's bus station for €7 (although be aware that there are only 3 buses a day which are all in the evening). *www.aena.es* will allow you to see live arrivals and departures, in English. For those without the web, the telephone number is ☎968 172000.

Destinations include: Barcelona, Madrid, Palma De Mallorca, Helsinki, Dublin, Shannon, Rome, Bergen, Oslo, Trondheim, Birminghan, Glasgow, Leeds, London (Stansted, Gatwick, Luton), Manchester, Manston (Kent), Nottingham, Southampton.

Airlines

✈ Jet 2
www.Jet2.com
☎ 902 020051

✈ My Travellite
www.mytravellite.com
☎ 902 020191

✈ Ryan Air
www.ryanair.com
☎ 807 220032

✈ Iberia
www.iberia.com
☎ 807 123456

✈ Flybe
www.flybe.com
☎ 00 44 13 922 685 28 (UK number only)

✈ BMI Baby
www.bmibaby.com
☎ 902 100737

Car Hire Companies
Centauro
www.centauro.net
☎   968 572185

Europa
www.europa–rentacar.es
☎   968 336523

Europ Car
www.europcar.es
☎   968 335546

Sol Mar
www.solmar.es
☎   968 335542

Where To Stay
Camping is available on the road towards Balsicas (Ctra Balsicas)
☎   968 191080

Pensión Nenico ★ ★
Calle Princípe, 10
☎   968 572901

Pensión El Lobo ★
Calle Doctor Pardo López, 26
☎   968 192739 or 968 573914

Santiago De La Ribera

Population: 3,500

Map Reference: E2 0.80°W, 37,80°N

Perhaps the most attractive of the Mar Menor resorts, Santiago de la Ribera sits on the shores of the Mar Menor directly in front of San Javier and the two are closely linked. Home to a superb marina area and some of the best restaurants in the region, it is no surprise that luxury villas and manicured gardens are the standard.

This resort is on the coast of the Mar Menor very close to San Javier airport. In fact you can frequently enjoy a free display from the airforce training school which shares the runway at San Javier. This town is very popular with the townies from Murcia at the weekends, especially in the summer – Santiago is a great place to go and have seafood and enjoy the sunshine.

The promenade at Santiago de la Ribera has been reconstructed. There are two restaurants located side–by–side on the beach. Restaurante Lonja Mar Menor is open for lunch and evening meals all year round. The Pescaderia–Restaurante Miguel is open all day in the high season but lunches only out–of–season. It also has a resident colony of cats who live under the wooden floorboards (I counted 15) and are very friendly if you are eating fish! Both establishments have fish shops attached.

Escursiones Joven Maria Dolores – offering daily boat trips to Islands in the Mar Menor ☎629 607047, only in high summer.

Tourist Office – Calle Padre Juan
☎ 968 571704
www.marmenor.net

Where To Stay
Pensión K–Hito ★ ★
Only open in summer, aircon
☎ 968 570002

Pensión Manida ★ ★
Calle Muñoz, 11
☎ 968 570011
www.hotelmanida.com

Hotel Albohera
☎ 968 335910
www.hotelalbohera.com

Pensión La Obrera ★ ★
Calle Zarandona, 7
☎ 968 570042
www.laobrera.com

Where To Eat
Bar Restaurante Lonja Mar Menor – Paseo Colón – excellent seafood, huge open freezers where you can select your fish, right on the seafront. It also has an excellent, though usually very busy, bar where you can have great seafood tapas. Next door there is Pescaderia–Restaurante Miguel.

San Pedro del Pinatar
Population: 16,700

Map Reference: F3 0.80°W, 37.81°N

Just south of Lo Pagan on the Mar Menor you'll find San Pedro del Pinatar. These two towns pretty much run into each other. You'll find a few majestic 19th century villas and also the Museo de Mar in Calle Lorenzo Noral.

Its local fiesta (fiesta patronal) is on 29th of June and they have a Flamenco festival in July.

ⓘ Tourist Office – Parque de los Reyes de España
☎ 968 182301
www.sanpedrodelpinatar.net

Ayuntamiento – Plaza Luis Molina, 1
☎   968 180661
Bus Station – Alalde José María Tárraga
☎   968 182942
Taxis – Calle Victor Pradera
☎   968 181760 or 968 180808 or 968 186996
Train station trains along the Mar Menor and to Balsicas
☎   968 580052

Where To Stay
Pensión Casa Lucrecia ★ ★
Calle Las Beatas, 21–22
☎   968 181928
See Lo Pagan for more information and places to stay.

Sierra Espuña
Map Reference: C2–C3 1.53°W, 37.80°N

The Sierra Espuña is a Parque Regional, which is right in the centre of the Murcia region, between the rivers Pliego and Guadalentín. It is actually an artificially planted forestry project which was started in 1891 to combat the deforestation which resutled in erosion and flash floods.

The park contains some of the higher peaks in Murcia, including the Espuña mountain (1585m), Pedro López (1566m) and Morrón Chico (1446m).

There are a couple of information centres in the park itself: Puerta Espuña and Las Alquerras. The park contains a number of different varieties of pine trees and many different types of wildlife including Montpellier snakes, butterflys and Barbary sheep.

It's usual to get to the park by car, from Alhama or Totana (the more adventurous can walk or go by bike from these towns). There are a vast variety of walks and cycle routes through the park which are best described in the book Descrubrir Sierra Espuña (from Natursport, ☎609 623061, *www.natursport.com* – this book can also be bought from the main bookshops in Murcia – see Murcia section).

Walking and cycling in the vast park area is becoming increasingly popular. It's a good idea to let someone know where you're going and when to expect you back as it is easy to become enveloped in the pine trees and lose your way. Wear appropriate clothing, take some food and water, expect the weather to change and take a good map.

For more information visit: *www.sierraespuna.com*

Locally there is also the town of Pliego, lying on one of the transhumance routes, used until recently to move livestock from summer to winter pastures.

Aljibe – Sierra Espuña

Where To Stay

Camping Sierra Espuña – El Berro
11 wooden lodges of different sizes with a camping area divided into plots. There's a swimming pool, café, playpen, barbecues, sports grounds, tennis courts, mini–golf, table tennis, public phones, 24–hour hot water, laundrette, fountains with drinking water, power points, first–aid box.

☎   968 668038
www.campingsierraespuna.com

Casa Rurales
La Tinaja, Las Palmeras, El Aljibe, El Limonar
☎   902 106600 – central agency Noratur

Casa Rural La Santa
Ctra Aledo, 7km
☎   968 421720

Where To Eat

The village of Berro has just over 100 inhabitants. It is situated at the altitude of 650m and has an array of services, such as restaurants, supermarkets, cafés, bakeries. Some of the best restaurants in the Sierra Espuña can be found here. It is also a great base for starting a walk or cycle ride.

Totana

Population: 24,700

Map Reference: D2 1.50ºW, 37.78ºN

One of the principal attractions of Totana is just outside town towards the Sierra Espuña. The Santuario de la Santa is nestled in a valley to the northwest of town, this 17th century monastery decadent in striking pink stands out against the green of the pine forest.

Back in the centre of town the area is known for pottery, there are a couple of shops specialising in selling local pieces, including Bellón on Paseo Ollerías and Ibero Alfar on Calle Tinajerías.

There are a number of other workshops out of town, between the N340 and the road to Mazarrón.

The local fiesta is on the 7th of January.

ⓘ Tourist Office – Avenida del General Aznar, 12
☎ 968 423902
www.ayto–totana.net, *www.totana.org* or *www.totana.com*

Ayuntamiento – Plaza De La Constitucion, 1
☎ 968 418151
Bus Station, Calle Juan Carlos I – buses to Murcia, Mazarrón and Lorca
☎ 968 425427
Train Station, Águilas – Murcia line, out to the south east of town.
☎ 968 425427

Where To Stay
Hotel Plaza ★
Plaza de la Constitución, 5
€45 per night
☎ 968 423112

Hotel los Camioneros ★ ★
N340, km 287
Just out of town towards Lorca, €39 per night
☎ 968 421037

Where To Eat
Tapas can be had on the Plaza de la Constitución. Also worth trying is Tara on Calle Santa Barbara and Cairo on Calle la Fuente.

- Casa Mariquita – Calle Canovas del Castillo, 8 – a well–known local restaurant specialising in home–made pickled chicken breast (Pechugas en Escabeche)
- Restaurante Plaza – Plaza de la Constitución, 5 – large restaurant with both local and international dishes.

Yecla

Population: 30,900

Map Reference: E6 1.12°W, 38.62°N

The northern most town of Murcia is Yecla (96 km north of Murcia). Yecla is one of the three wine producing regions with its own DOC in Murcia (the other two being Bullas and Jumilla). The name Yecla comes from the Arab word Yakka.

Up on the hill you'll find the Santuario de la Purísima Concepcion, which offers great views of the town and surrounding areas. There is also a castle, Castillo de Yecla, from the 14th century. There are many churches in the town. The old town is quite beautiful but rather short on bars, restaurants and cafes.

The principal industry is the manufacture of furniture, with 40 furniture shops along one road alone.

The fiesta of San Isidro is in the middle of May and their Fiesta Patronales is in December.

ⓘ Tourist office
☎   958 754104

Ayuntamiento – Plaza Mayor
☎   968 751135 or 968 718000
www.ayuntamientoyecla.com

Taxis
☎616 373939 ☎646 913307 ☎968 791216
Useful website: *www.yeclaserve.com*

Where To Eat
There are restaurants around the town, you might want to try Restaurante La Paz – Avenida La Paz, 180

Where To Stay
Hotel Avenida
Calle San Pasqual, 3
€48 per night
☎ 968 751215

Hotel La Paz
Avenida de la Paz, 180
€72 per night
☎ 968 751350

Facts

Culture

Reading the history books you'd be forgiven for thinking Murcia doesn't actually exist. From the Romans, to the Muslims, the Visigoths to the Spanish Inquisistion, Murcia remains resolutely unmentioned. Murcia's cultural heritage bears an impression of old battles and recent political machinations; however, it remains clearly removed from the limelight. Signs of the influence of all of these invaders and aggressors litter the whole region – from aqueducts, castles, fortifications and Roman roads lined with olive trees to the stunning architecture of the grand buildings in the cities.

Murcia is a friendly region, a warm "Buenos Dias" upon entering a shop or restaurant is uttered to all, followed by an "Adios" or "Hasta Luego" upon departure. At the coast, they don't expect visitors to speak much Spanish, however in the villages a lack of Spanish can create difficulties as few rural Spaniards learn English.

The Murcianos are a gregarious bunch, taking great care to include children and the older generations in their social activities. They enjoy making an effort in their appearance. A walk around the Murcian capital on a summer's Saturday evening will show a decadence in dress that us Brits generally reserve for weddings! Even the children will be dressed in their finery.

Murcians works on the same timetable as most of the rest of Spain – relaxed! The heat for most of the year encourages a long lunch break, followed by chatting and snoozing during the afternoon (siesta). The shops mostly close between 2pm and 5pm for most of the year, reopening at 5pm and staying open until 8 or 9pm.

During the hottest months Murcianos take advantage of the cooler evenings, sitting and chatting outside till well past midnight. It's not uncommon to see young children racing round outside restaurants at 2am, while their parents and extended family drink slowly and cool down.

In August Murcianos take a well needed 1 month holiday. Many shops and restaurants (outside of the tourist destinations) will shut down or work reduced hours, while their Murciano proprietors enjoy the beaches and the mountains.

Transport

Road Network

Murcia has an excellent network of motorways and main roads. Murcia, Águilas, Jumilla, the Mar Menor and Cartagena are all mostly well interlinked. A new motorway program is underway to improve the notoriously slow progress around the North of Cartagena, and eventually to link through to Águilas.

Jeremy Clarkson would be delighted to hear that, at this moment, there are no toll motorways in Murcia – the tolls start as soon as you cross the border into Alicante province and will cost a few Euros to get to Alicante airport, for example. Be warned that Gatsos (speed cameras) were introduced in 2005 – and that includes Murcia – the question remains whether the locals will treat it as an 'important law' (and therefore to be obeyed strictly) or an 'unimportant law' (such as no smoking in airport terminals).

Airports

Murcia's only international airport is at San Javier (see San Javier section for full details). However, the regional government has recognised that the 4–belt, 5–jet capacity of the airport is barely adequate for the 54 golf complexes that will soon be covering every corner of the region. Whilst Corvera aiport (see below) is (still) in the planning process, San Javier has had another runway built and the terminal and car parking facilities have been expanded.

A new airport has been planned to the south of Corvera. This will be closer to the city of Murcia itself (some 20km to the south) and will rival Alicante's El Altet and Málaga for the capacity, duty free shopping and range of fast food franchises. However, as with many projects in the region, it is behind schedule, originally slated to open in 2006, there is still no sign of building, although dozens of golf complexes have sprung up around it in anticipation. (Ironincally, we note in the local press that one of the local golf complexes was complaining the authorities that they would be in the flight path of the new airport – at the same time as proclaiming proximity to the airport as one of the virtues of buying a house in that housing estate…)

Alternative airports for Murcia are, in order of convenience, Alicante (El Altet), Almería and, if you want the best connectivity, Madrid (Barajas). From Murcia city, with no traffic and with a lead foot, you can get to Alicante in an hour, Almería in two and Madrid in four hours.

Trains

As it stands today, Murcia is not particularly well–served by trains. You are in luck if you want to travel between Cartegena and Murcia and between Águilas and Murcia. The train service to Madrid uses the older TALGO / ALTARIA diesel electric trains and so the journey takes some 4 hours. There is also a FEVE line that trundles between Cartagena and Los Nietos (on the Mar Menor near Los Alcázares) – *www.feve.es*.

The super–fast AVE trains (called 'patos' locally) won't be throughout Murcia much before 2020. You can check timetables and buy tickets on the RENFE web site: *www.renfe.es*. Prices are refreshingly reasonable compared to the shocking standard prices in the UK. For example, a return ticket from Murcia to Madrid is currently only €76, and Cartegena to Murcia return is €27 return.

Buses

Buses in Murcia make up for the lack of train connections around the region. From Murcia's main bus station (see the Murcia town section for details), you can get buses to just about anywhere in the country. For example, if you wanted to go to Málaga by train, you would have to go almost all the way into Madrid and then back down south to the coast. In contrast there are buses from Murcia going straight there. The long–distance coaches are good value, for example a return ticket from Murcia to Madrid is €43.

Most long distance routes are serviced by the ALSA bus company: *www.alsa.es*. For buses around the region, you can try Latbus ☎968 250088 and *www.latbus.com*.

However, the services between outlying towns could hardly be called frequent. For example, there are only 3 buses a day during the week from Fuente Álamo into Murcia and none on Sunday. If you do ever see such a bus, the journey would only cost you €2.20.

Taxis

For getting around within a city such as Murcia or Cartagena, assuming you don't want to walk, a taxi can be a reasonable option. You want to look for taxis from a taxi rank or one that you have phoned in advance – see individual town entries in this book for specifics.

Taxis are certainly very reasonably priced per kilometre, but as soon as you start getting out of the city, then the kilometres start to mount. There are plenty of travellers who have bagged a bargain basement flight to 'Murcia' and then caught a cab into town only to find that it would probably have been cheaper to hire a car for the weekend.

Car Rental

Unless you live full–time in Spain and have bought your own wheels, car rental is probably the most cost–effective way of getting around Murcia. For week–long rentals you can often get a small car for as little as €12 a day. See the San Javier section for a list of the rental companies operating locally.

Language

The language in Murcia is Castilian Spanish – the standard Spanish you'd be taught in school (not Catalan).

However, the Spanish spoken in Murcia is quite different from other areas of Spain. "Murciano" tends to eliminate many syllable–final consonants and to emphasise regional vocabulary, much of which is derived from old Arabic words. Some Murcian countryfolk still speak a separate dialect, called Panocho, which is virtually unintelligible to speakers of standard Castilian Spanish.

What you'll most likely notice is the lack of "s" at the end of many words, for example "do" instead "dos" (two).

English	Spanish	Pronunciation
Spanish	*español*	(es–pahn–YOL)
Spanish (Castilian)	*castellano*	(kah–steh–YAH–no)
Hello, hi	*Hola*	(OH–la)
Goodbye	*Adiós*	(ahdy–OS)
Please	*por favor*	(pore faah–VOR–e)
Thank you	*Gracias*	(GRA–thyahs)
Sorry	*perdón*	(pair–DON)
That (thing)	*eso*	(EH–saw)
How much?	*cuánto*	(KWAHN–to)
For example,...	*por ejemplo,...*	(pore eh–HEM–ploh)
English	*inglés*	(ing–GLESS)
Yes	*sí*	(see)
No	*no*	(noh)
I don't understand	*no entiendo*	(noh en–tYEN–do)
Where's the bathroom?	*¿dónde está el baño?*	(DON–deh es–TAH el BA–nyo)
Cheers! (toast)	*¡salud!*	(sah–LOOTHE)
Do you speak English?	*¿habla usted inglés?*	(AH–blah oos–TED ing–GLESS)

Useful Web Links

Spanish phrases with audio:
www.quiz–buddy.com/spanish_phrases_with_audio.html
Dictionary:
www.diccionarios.com
Spanish lessons online:
http://en.wikibooks.org/wiki/spanish

To Buy

We have tried lots of Spanish language CDs, videos and books and we've found that the best, by far, are from Michel Thomas.

Complete 8 course CD set:
www.amazon.co.uk/exec/obidos/ASIN/0340780673/leanmarketing–21

Language Builder:
www.amazon.co.uk/exec/obidos/ASIN/0340789719/leanmarketing–21

Advanced Course:
www.amazon.co.uk/exec/obidos/ASIN/0340887036/leanmarketing–21

To accompany the CDs we recommend "501 Spanish Verbs":
www.amazon.co.uk/exec/obidos/ASIN/0764124285/leanmarketing–21

The biggest and the best Spanish Dictionary (it's very heavy):
www.amazon.co.uk/exec/obidos/ASIN/0007155786/leanmarketing–21

Spanish Grammar Guide:
www.amazon.co.uk/exec/obidos/ASIN/0071422706/leanmarketing–21

Language Schools
Instituto Cervantes, is an organisation that lists over 1700 Spanish courses in Spain. Take a look here: *http://eee.cervantes.es*

The following Instituto Cervantes accredited school in Murcia is worth trying:

ABACO Instituto Hispánico de Murcia, Calle Enrique Villar, 13
☎   968 900 325
www.ihdemu.com

Flora and Fauna

The best website for flora and fauna in the region is:
www.regmurcia.com/servlet/integra.servlets.ServletLink?sit=c|365|m|1039

Copy the link exactly, this will get you straight to the correct section. There are great photographs, excellent descriptions and useful geological information, all in Spanish.

Mammals

Weasels are just about everywhere in the region. Martens can be found mostly in the mountains, with Wild Cats in the Sierra Espuña and the Sierra de Moratalla and other mountain forests. You'll find badgers around the areas of Lorca, Águilas and Mazarrón. Otters are very rare but can be seen near the embalses of Cenajo and Mulata and the rivers Benamor and Quípar. At the smaller end of the scale are garden dormouse and red squirrels.

JABALÍ

Walking along the rambla at the back of our caves (on the way to the bar in the village), with our 3 teenage nephews we were accompanied by a baby wild boar (Jabalí). The tiny wild boar cheerfully followed around our ankles, snuffling and playing with the boys, chasing after sticks that were thrown for it, while we adults nervously watched for its larger mother to appear – tusks bared! Luckily the baby got bored and wandered off. We got a large brandy.

Barbary sheep (Arrui or Muflón del Atlas) can be spotted in the Sierra Espuña if you're very lucky. Wild Boar (Jabalí) can be found around Águilas, Mazarrón, Sierra de Carrascoy and the Mar Menor.

And in every village a cacophony of cats can be found at the bakery door with a pack of dogs cheerfully wandering the streets and making friends with visitors.

SIERRA ESPUÑA

While driving to the top of the Sierra Espuña on a bright January afternoon, we were shocked to see before us in the road a beautiful Barbary sheep staring at us, resplendent with long antlers. We stopped and watched it run into the undergrowth where it joined a family of about 30. Later that same trip we spotted the entire family grazing on the hillside.

Birds

Pied Wagtails can be found in patches throughout the region, Great Bustards, Blackbirds and Long Tailed Tits are just about everywhere. Flamingoes live in Salinas del San Pedro del Pinatar; Shelduks in Embalse de Santomera, Salinas del San Pedro del Pinatar and Salinas del Marchamalo; Stone Curlews in Saladares del Guadalentín; Little Owls, Eurasian Eagle Owls mostly in the mountains.

Hoopoes, Partridges, Barn Owls, Golden Orioles (incredibly beautiful), Golden Eagles, Common Buzzards, Peregrine Falcons (Sierra de Cartagena, Mazarrón and Sierra de Almenara), Bonelli's Eagles (Sierra del Altiplano, Calblanque and Peña del Águila) and Eurasian Kestrels can also be found here.

SQUATTERS

During the early stages of our building work, when we were travelling back and forth, we purchased a big bag of gravel. You know, those large industrial, 1 tonne nylon bags. We left it mostly full and returned 6 weeks later to find our neighbour, David, quietly sneaking up on it, encouraging us to come over and take a peek. Inside was a lovely birds nest, beautifully crafted with a tiny pied–wagtail proprietorially protecting three blue eggs.

So we bought another bag of gravel and allowed the birds to hatch.

This wasn't our only encounter with birds. Barn Swallows apparently love caves. We spent two weeks in June, in a mad game of hide and seek, afraid to open the door to the cave house in case the swallows rushed in on us.

On the three or four occasions when they managed to take siege of the cave house, we would then spend a hot and frustrated couple of hours, trying to negotiate their retreat.

They always worked in pairs, swooping together and landing gracefully on our drying rack (a bamboo pole used for hanging mint and camomile), calling cheerfully with their veet–veet song!

You can recognise these beautiful interlopers by their reddish brown face, cream chest and black back with a long forked tail.

Reptiles

The Horseshoe Whip Snake, around 1 metre long can be found throughout the region, mostly around Yecla; the Viperine Water Snake grows to 50–80cm and is normally found near water; Montpellier Snakes, upto 2 metres in length, can be found around the region, they eat insects and small mammals.

Lataste's Viper at 50cm has very fast movement and is found in wooded areas. The Ladder Snake found around the whole region, in woods and natural areas, grows to about 1 metre.

Jewelled lacertas (eyed lizard), around 60cm at their largest, can be found in the northwest of the region; Bedriaga's Skink which looks a bit like a snake, but with short legs and a very cylindrical body is fairly small, can be found around the Mar Menor. Lizard Podarcis Hispanica, which are typically only 5cm long, can be found around the whole region. They were almost extinct until 1970 when they were reintroduced.

Tortoise (Testudo graeca) from North Africa, can be found around most of the region and Mediterranean Pond Turtles at 15cm in length can too.

Turkish Geckos or Salamancas are common in the whole region, especially, it seems, in our cave house.

THE SLITHERING INNER TUBE

While driving along the road near Corvera we drove over what we thought was a bicycle inner tube, kerdunk, kerdunk, only to notice as we drove away that the "inner tube" also slithered away into the grass. We believe it was a Montpellier snake, fairly common in the region.

Amphibians

The Spanish Ribbed Newt usually around 20cm though can grow upto 32cm is found near Yecla; European toad whose male carries the fertilized eggs wrapped around its hind legs until they hatch, are very small (only 4cm); Natterjack Toads and Common Toads are common around most of the region too.

The Mediterranean Treefrog and Iberian Spadefoot Toad are found in the north of the region while the Spanish Painted Frog at just 7cm and the tiny Common Parsley Frog are dotted around the entire region.

Salamandra Salamandra, the largest in the family, prefers woodland. It has a shiny black body, with yellow splashes and is found only in the northwest.

Fish

The following seafish are all common: Grouper (up to 1.4 m), Striped Sea Bream (30cm), Gilthead Sea Bream (60 cm), Atlantic mackerel (up to 60 cm), Atlantic Horse Mackerel (40 cm) and Fartet (4 cm).

Trees & Herbs

Trees – Small–leaved Elm, White Poplar, Apricot (Cieza), Plum (North–West), Peach (North and North–West), Strawberry (Mula and Segura valleys), Walnut, Almond, Carrascoy Pine, Carob, Stone Pine and Olive.

RIPE FOR THE PICKING

Take a walk along any rambla in the springtime and you'll find a huge array of herbs just waiting to be picked. Often you'll see a family returning from their afternoon paseo with bunches of rosemary.

Chumbo – can reach upto 2m in height, with beautiful flowers and wonderful fruit, though take care when harvesting them, the chumbos tree is also known as the prickly pear. They grow throughout the region and are often used as a natural waste eater!

Vitis vinífera – vines, to make grapes that make wine! There are a number of varieties –including Monastrell, Garnacha Tinta and Cencibel, Tempranillo to make the red wines and Macabe and Airén for the white wines. They are also cultivating a Cabernet Sauvignon. The grapes have other properties too – including as a tonic, a decongestant and a laxative, now who told us wine was good for you! The region is also home to some rare but beautiful flowers including the Butterfly Orchid, Sea Daffodil and Sea Holly.

Actvities

Fiestas

The Murcian enthusiasm for Fiestas rivals the Madrileños (Madrid inhabitants). Each town or village has its own Patrimonio day, which you can find by looking on a calendar. You can read through the town guides to find specific fiestas but below are some of the more well–known ones of the region.

January

- Los Reyes – the Three Wise Men – on 6th January the Spanish children receive their Christmas gifts. Most towns and villages will do something special in social clubs and town squares. Murcia and Cartagena have extra special fiestas. Look out for the televised celebrations of Madrid with massive floats, and the three kings parading through the city.
- Carnaval de Águilas – Águilas
- Fiestas de San Sebastián – Ricote

February

- Carnaval – Cabezo de Torres
- Carnaval – Cartagena
- Carnaval – Mar Menor – San Pedro del Pinatar, San Javier and Los Alcázares alternately
- San Blas de San Javier Romeria – San Javier

March

- Semana Santa – Easter Week – being a mainly Catholic country, Easter is a huge celebration. All towns and villages will hold celebrations, with at least 3 or 4 working days lost. Some of the best festivities can be found in Cartagena, Jumilla, Murcia and Moratalla.

April

- Fiesta de la Primavera (Spring festival) in Murcia includes: Bando de la Huerta (Orchard procession) and Entierra de la Sardina (Burial of the Sardine)

- Certamen Internacional de Tunas Costa Calida is an international music festival. Running since 1988, tunas (student music groups) gather from all over the world to perform. There are many night performances and street concerts to attend. Usually takes place at the end of April.

ONLY VISITING ONCE?
Then make sure you come for Spring Festival. The flights will be cheaper (after Easter holidays), the weather should be great (not too hot, plenty of sunshine) and the partying is not to be missed. The floats, costumes, excitement and general friendliness in the city, will ensure you have a great time. Park on the outskirts of the city, walk in along the river and enjoy Murcia doing its thing!

May
- Santisima y Vera Cruz – Caravaca

June
- Jazz Festival – San Javier
- Feria Sevillana – Mar Menor
- San Juan – all towns and villages

July
- Jazz Festival – San Javier
- Virgen Del Carmen – Cartagena
- Santiago Apostle – Cartagena

August
- San Gines de la Jara Procession – San Gines
- Festival of International Theatre, Music and Dance – San Javier
- Mar Menor Folk Festival – San Pedro del Pinatar and Lo Pagán
- Fiesta de la Vendimia in Jumilla with a wine fountain to celebrate the wine harvest.

September
- Murcia September Fair: Moors & Christians – Murcia
- "Tunas" Folk Music Festival – Murcia
- Mediterranean Folklore Festival – Murcia
- Romans & Carthaginians – Cartagena
- Rice Festival, celebrating the harvest of the rice, the usual partying and bull fights – Calasparra

October
- Regional Horse Fair – Caravaca

November
- Romería de San Clemente – Lorca

December
- Fiestas Mayores – San Javier
- Tours of the Natives (Belenes) – Yecla

Exact dates cannot be given for many of the above fiestas due to ever changing dates. If you want to plan your holiday/trip at fiesta time then contact the Murcia tourist office for exact dates.

ⓘ Murcia Tourist Office

☎ 00 34 902 101070

Email: *turinfo@carm.es*

How To Fiesta
Fiestas are serious business in Murcia. It's important that you know when your local fiesta (fiesta patronal) is – check in your local teleclub or bar. Preparations start weeks in advance (depending upon the scale of the celebrations intended) with roles assigned for many of the villagers.

Usually the festivities are spread over a week or even more, with a program of activities planned. In many bars you'll find a guide to these activities along with lots of adverts from local traders.

For larger fiestas, the lights will go up in the streets a few weeks ahead, and often a marquee will be erected in the town square. Sometimes there will be competitions – football, sport, fruit and vegetable growing and, of course, the paella cooking.

Never expect evening festivities to begin much before 10pm or finish much earlier than 6am.

Sport

The tourist offices in the towns, in Murcia city or on the Internet can provide more information about the many sporting activities in the region, including hiking, walking, cycling, riding, wind surfing, water skiing, scuba diving, bird watching or golfing. We outline some of the more popular ones below. For sports equipment in general, you can try the El Corte Inglés department store (Murcia and Cartagena) and the newly–opened Decathlon sports supermarket just off the A–7 motorway coming into Cartagena. These two shops combined provide supplies for just about everything from shooting to scuba, but, as always, specialist shops will offer more choice.

Walking, Trekking & Hiking

With its large tracts of wilderness, mountains, coasts, cliffs and forests, Murcia offers unrivalled opportunities for treks – short half day walks or longer excursions.

There is an extensive network of long distance walks throughout Spain, with a number crossing into Murcia. These are called the senderos de Gran Recorrido (GRs). We have the GR7 all the way from Andorra, as well as many shorter footpaths called the senderos de Pequeño Recorrido (PRs).

The best books, covering the whole of the region are a range from Natursport – *www.natursport.com* – wich can be bought online or from Murcia city (see the city guide pages for the local bookshop). Their publications inlcude walking and cycling routes along the River Segura, into the Sierra Espuña and along the miles of coast. For hiking boots and equipment sold by somebody who actually *uses* the kit they sell, try SUR, Calle Vara de Rey 5, Murcia ☎968 22 08 48 – good prices and selection.

The Federación de Orientación de la Región de Murcia *www.form–orientacion.com* organises orienteering in the region.

Horse Riding
La Manga – El Rancho de la Fuente

La Manga Club has its own Equestrian Centre at El Rancho de la Fuente. The Centre offers riding lessons for all standards. More accomplished riders can trek through the local foothills of the Calblanque or along the beach coves of Cala Reona. A one hour climb of the La Fuente hills to the summit will reveal splendid views of the Mediterranean and the Mar Menor.
☎ 968 137239

Picadero Pascualón – Moratalla, towards Camping de la Puerta
☎ 968 706078 or 616 142638

Los Belones – Cuadras el Puntal – Campo del Golf
☎ 636 067218

Club Hípico del Mediterráneo – Carretera molinos Marfagones
☎ 968 534410

Totana – La Charca – Poto
☎ 968 420006 (also Puerto Mazarrón)

Los Almagros – Complejo Rural (a few km North of the village – signposeted on East exit from village) – Jorge
☎ 968 220848

Cycling
Spain is well known for producing some of the best cyclists in Europe and if you go out on the Murcian roads on any Sunday morning, you will see why. Cycling is a very popular sport, in groups as well as individually. If you are interested in joining a club you can get in touch with the Murcia branch of the Federación de Ciclismo on ☎968 302846.

The Noratur books are again a great buy – *www.noratur.com*

Gliding, Paragliding and Skydiving

Extreme aerial sports are very active in Murcia – especially paragliding. Get in touch with Federación Deportes Aéreos de al Región de Murcia: *www.famur.org* for details or phone ☎868 910796.

Shooting

The main target shooting club network in Spain is Real Federación Española de Tiro Olímpico – don't worry you don't need to be an Olympian to join – has its central branch just outside Murcia city, towards Molina de Segura. Annual membership is €150, plus a joining fee – this may seem rather steep, but consider that this does include insurance plus access to a number of ranges that provide for trap shooting, pistol and smallbore. (We have yet to find a long fullbore range to rival Bisley, etc.) Contact them at ☎968 430194.

There are also private clubs providing clay and target shooting facilities. Target (paper punching) is available for a €100 annual membership just outside Corvera on the road to Baños y Mendigo (run by Armería del Carmen in Murcia – ☎968 251152).

If you are interested in hunting, try the Federación de Caza de la Región de Murcia: *www.federacioncaza.com*

The laws in Spain regarding sports shooting can be found here: *www.wfsa.net/intl_leg/leg_spain.htm*

In practice, there are two ways to to get a Spanish firearms license. If you already had one elsewhere in Europe (e.g. in the UK), the easiest way to get your Spanish license is to get your resident's permit (*residencia*) and take that along with your permit from the other EU country down to your nearest licensing department (*intervención de armas*) of the Guardia Civil. A few months later, if everything checks out OK, you should be able to pick up your Spanish equivalent permit. If you don't have a permit from another EU country, you have to do some swotting in Spanish to be able to answer a multiple choice test which is picked from 400 questions that are helpfully posted, with answers, on the Guardia Civil web site.

For shooting provisions, there are gunsmiths (*amrerías*) in just about every major town, but the best we have found is in Murcia – Armería de Carmen – Calle Floridablanca, 24 – ☎968 25 11 52. They also have a small branch in Cartagena – Avenida de America, 8 – 968 52 18 57.

Go Karts
There are a number of go–kart tracks in the region. One of the best and most professional is in Bullas. Prices range from €6 for children for 10 minutes to €15 for a larger kart for adults for a 10 minute drive. Chicano–Kart – Paraje "Cabeza Gorda" ☎699 907013. Also try the Complejo Rural, North of Los Almagros – €10 for 10 minutes for adults.

And for indoor Karting try Murcia Kart, Carretera de Madrid, 388, Cabezo Cortao ☎687 482590, very near Murcia city centre.

Scuba
Murcia is a great place to learn and explore scuba diving. The Mar Menor's shallow, calm and warm waters are great for beginners and the Mediterranean itself has loads of opportunities once you've got your certificate. The Federación de Actividades Subacuáticas de la Región de Murcia – *www.fasrm.com* – provides a central point of contact for most clubs in the region. Also, have a look at the PADI web site for acredited dive centres in Murcia: *www.padi.com*.

Around the whole Mar Menor region there are extensive beaches used for diving – el Mojón beach, Torre Derribada, La Llana, Las Salinas, Barraca Quemada and Punto de Algas – all in the Salinas Regional Park. The seabed offers a surprising range of attractive sands and the remains of Roman shipwrecks.

On the Med, all along the south coast there are Scuba clubs.

Águilas – La Almadraba, Calle Ernest Hemingway, 13 (Calabardina)
☎   968 419632

Cabo de Palos – Islas Hormigas Club
☎   968 145530

Cabo de Palos – Planeta Azul – PADI Dive Centre
☎   968 564532

La Azohía – Andrómeda
☎ 968 150328

La Manga – Mundo Activo – PADI Dive Centre
☎ 968 337087

La Manga – Deep Impact Diving Center – PADI Dive Centre
☎ 968337220

Puerto de Mazarrón – Zoea, Plaza del Mar, 20– PADI Dive Centre
☎ 968 154006

Scuba Diving Villa de San Pedro
☎ 676 745022
www.buceosanpedro.com

Scuba Diving Pinatar
☎ 699 121523
www.caspinatar.com

Scuba Diving Turkana
☎ 617 355636
www.turkana.org

For gear, there are scuba shops around in Puerto Mazarrón and La Manga. However, the best we have found is in Murcia – Armería de Carmen (yes, we know it's a gunsmith, they also sell fishing tackle!) – Calle Floridablanca, 24 – 968 25 11 52. They also have a small branch in Cartagena – Avenida de America, 8 – 968 52 18 57.

Watersports
Windsurfers will love La Mota beach, a completely natural course for speed, taking advantage of the wind without taking any risks.

Throughout the year, early in the morning the Mar Menor is a mirror, where canoeing is a safe sport for any age.

La Manga – Manga Surf
☎ 968 145331
www.mangasurf.com

Nautical Sports Clubs San Pedro
☎ 968 182678
www.puertosanpedro.com

Nautical Sports Clubs San Pedro
☎ 968 186969
www.clubnauticolopagan.com

Canoeing School
☎ 968 187260

Fishing
For local fishing clubs, contacts and legislation, get in touch with the Federación de Pesca y Casting

☎ 968 221012
www.fepyc.es

For the third time, we have to mention Armería de Carmen (not only the best gunsmith and scuba gear, but also the best fishing tackle) – Calle Floridablanca, 24 – 968 25 11 52. They also have a small branch in Cartagena – Avenida de America, 8 – 968 52 18 57.

Sailing
Murcia offers a good variety of sailing, with the shallow Mar Menor being great for beginners and the Mediterranean itself for the more experienced sailor. Sailing as a sport in Murcia comes under the umbrella of the Federación de Vela de la Región de Murcia: *www.fvrm.es*

Águilas – Club Náutico de Águilas. Paseo de la Parra, 44
☎ 968 411951
www.cnaguilas.com

Cartagena – Club Náutico, Puerto Maritima
☎ 968 133355
www.rcrct.net

La Manga – Manga Surf
☎ 968 145331
www.mangasurf.com

Mazarrón – Club de Regatas de Mazarrón, Calle Cabezo de Cebada
☎ 968 594011
www.serconet.com/usr/chicoyij

Santiago de la Ribera – Club de Regatas Santiago de la Ribera, Paseo de Colón
☎ 968 570250

Lo Pagán – Club Náutico Lo Pagán
☎ 968 186969
www.clubnauticolopagan.com

Los Neitos – Club Náutico Los Nietos
☎ 968 133300
www.cnlosnietos.com

Golf

Unless you have been living in a cave for the past few years, you are probably aware that Murcia is a golf mecca – in fact, even most troglodytes and hermits are fully aware of this, too.

La Manga – Perhaps the biggest golf complex in the whole region, centred around the Hotel Hyatt Regency. The north course is a 71 par layout, where precision, rather than length is required. The south course is located in the centre of the valley and can be enjoyed by golfers of all standards, and is a 72 par course.

☎ 968 331234
www.lamangaclub.com

Polaris World (near Torre Pacheco)
Course designed by Jack Niklaus.
☎ 902 203021
www.polarisworld.com/03/index.htm (English Version)

Torre Pacheco
☎ 968 579037
www.golftorrepacheco.com

Molina de Segura
☎ 968 648152
www.golfaltorreal.es

Fuente Álamo – Hacienda del Álamo
☎ 968 044417
www.haciendadelalamo.com

Baños y Mendigo – Mosa Trajectum
☎ 968 60 72 09
www.mosatrajectum.com

Health & Beauty
Mud is famous for its beauty and curative qualities. The muds of Las Charcas and Lo Pagan are particularly good due to the high salination of the waters of the Mar Menor. When the mud is applied to the skin it is reputed to have a great therapeutic value for all types of ailments, including: rheumatism, arthritis, gout, skin disorders and bone fractures.

Spa Aguas Salinas
☎ 968 184136
www.aguassalinas.com

Thalassotherapy Barceló Lodomar
☎ 968 186802
www.barcelo.com

Geocaching: What to do when it's too cold to go to the beach

Murcia has 320 days of sunshine a year. Right now, as I write this, it's snowing here (in February), only half an hour away from the Mar Menor. So, whilst Murcia's weather is usually some of the best in Europe, there are times when going for a swim in the sea is definitely out.

Murcia is blessed with fantastic countryside and one of the best ways to get out to places, that you would otherwise only wonder about as you drive by on the motorway, is a new pursuit called 'geocaching'. Geocaching came about when gadget freaks wanted an excuse to go out and buy the, then, newfangled latest gizmo, a handheld GPS receiver. On 1st May 2000, the U.S. government switched their satellites on to a new, higher accuracy service for civilians. What this meant was that those hand–held GPS gadgets could now place themselves on the earth to within a dozen metres or so of accuracy. Great. Now what? Nice for surveyors, great for shipping and aviation, but what's the hobbyist going to do with the gadget? Geocaching, that's what!

"Where is it?" – Fuggles, Dani and Marcus look for the cache

Geocaching is, basically, hiding things in interesting places around the globe and publishing your stash or 'cache' on a web site: *www.geocaching.com*. On this web site, which is free to browse and join up as a member (membership necessary to publish a cache), you can search for all caches near a town, near your home, in a country, etc. It's great fun for families, especially, since it gets everybody outdoors and it's educational too (mapping, nature, etc.)

Murcia has about 20 caches at the moment, and that number is rising quickly. They are mostly in places of great natural beauty, perhaps with sea views or really off the beaten track. There are caches near Cartagena, near Murcia, Mazarrón and even way off in the mountains on the Almería border.

So this is a really expensive hobby, right? Not really, the GPS receivers can now cost as little as a good pair of hiking boots. Of course, as with all gadgets, you can spend more (up to €500 for an all–singing, all–dancing, colour display model with built–in maps, electronic compass and barometric altimeter (gadget freaks can stop drooling now)). Garmin and Magellen are the makes to look for when shopping. The other things you will need are those that every sensible hiker owns anyway: good boots with ankle support, water bottles, a map pocket and a mobile phone in case of emergencies. A camera, spare pen and a gonk will help, too. I'll explain why later.

For each published cache there will be, at a minimum, coordinates of the cache that you can punch into the GPS receiver to use as your guide to the hidden treasure. There will usually be a general description of the area, what kind of things were originally stored in the cache and usually some clues on how to get to the cache, such as where to park and marked footpaths to follow. Often the cache listing includes a 'spoiler' which spells out exactly how to find the cache, but needs to be deciphered by hand so you don't spoil your fun unless you really want to give up looking.

Remember that the GPS receivers are great, but not perfect. You will get very close to the spot with the help of the gizmo, but the next fun part is grubbing around under rocks and around trees to find the cache itself, which is usually hidden away from prying eyes. When you get to the cache, you will often find a Tupperware or metal container (usually an old army–surplus ammo box), which is clearly marked as being a geocache. Inside you will find a log book where you can make a note of your visit (remember the pen?) and some knickknacks. The protocol is to swap knickknacks (remember the gonk?) and take a photo of you on your visit (remember the camera?). When you are done, seal up and hide the cache back as you found it. When you get back to the house, you can record your visit to the cache, describing your experience, giving some hints or tips for future visitors, and even upload that photo you took while you were there!

We look forward to you visiting our caches and us finding yours!

The Game of Caliche

The game of *caliche* is particular to the Murcia / Levante region of Spain, based on a nationally–played game called *herrón*. If you, as we did, look up *caliche* in the English–Spanish dictionary (after seeing it in the itinerary for the local fiesta), you might be confused or even horrified. *Caliche* (in our 4 inch thick Collins mega–dictionary) means 'saltpetre', or *echar un caliche* means something really quite surprising, and I'm not going to reproduce the translation here (we were getting prepared to watch from a distance!).

Caliche is a game rather like skittles in Britain. 'Rather' as in very loosely indeed. It is played on a flat surface (say, the road outside your local *teleclub*) that is 35m long and 6m wide. A wooden baton (called the *caliche*), 20cm long and 3cm diameter is placed 7m from the end of the field. A 2cm disk (*moneda*) is placed on top of the baton. The end of the field is blocked off with a stout table or similar, turned on its side to stop the *moneo* disks which you throw at the baton. A *moneo* is a weighty metal disk of 8cm diameter (could be square, too) and about 2mm thick.

The objective of the game is to throw the *moneo* at the *caliche* in such a way as the *moneda* and *moneo* end up as close as possible to each other (after displacing the *moneo* from the *caliche*.)

The game is usually played with two teams of two. Each game has 8 throws, 4 per team and 2 per player. For a throw to be considered valid, the *moneda* must end up closer to the *moneo* than the *caliche*. If the *moneo* ends up nearer the *caliche*, the throw was invalid and is called a '*ganga*'.

A *ganga* throw can also be considered valid (made into a *ganga válida*) in the following way. You can throw another *moneo* down the field with a view to getting that one to land closer to the *moneda* than the *caliche*, or throwing another *moneo* in order to move the *caliche* so that the *moneo* you threw initially is now closer to the *moneda* than the *caliche*. If the player manages to achieve one of these 'validation moves', the throw is said to be *arrimar* or *arrestar*.

If, after throwing the second *moneo* after a *ganga* throw, you still don't have a valid throw, there is one last option to validate your throw. The *caliche* and *moneda* get put back in their place in the centre line of the field and 7m from the end board. Once set up, the team that throws first has up to 4 opportunities to overturn the *caliche* and make a *ganga*. If so, the team that throws second will have to make a *ganga válida* to gain a point.

The teams take turns to play first. Typically a match comprises 12 or 20 rounds (*manos*). A point is gained by each the team winning the *mano*.

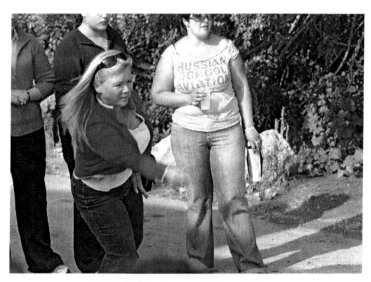

Debbie playing Caliche with the neighbours

Markets

There are plenty of markets around. Most towns have a particular market day, some of which are included here. The markets in Murcia sell everything from fruit and veg, fish and meat to hair dryers and CDs.

Monday
San Pedro del Pinatar
Caravaca de la Cruz

Tuesday
Alhama de Murcia
Los Alcázeres
La Union
Jumilla
Molina de Segura

Wednesday
Cartagena
Alcantarilla
Cieza
Santiago de la Ribera
Totana
Yecla

Thursday
Murcia
San Javier
Lorca

Friday
Cartagena
El Algar

Saturday
Águilas
Mazarrón
Torre Pacheco
Molina de Segura
Fuente Alamo

Sunday
Puerto Mazarrón
Purias
Cabo de Palos

Beaches

The following beaches are amongst the most beautiful in the region:

1. Villa Nanitos – near the mud baths of San Pedro del Pinatar, with various sporting facilities such as wind surfing, volley ball, kayaking and waterskiing.
2. La Llana – long, sandy, blue flag beach, with foot showers during the main season. Mild water, with some waves in parts.
3. El Espejo – another blue flag, sandy beach on the Mar Menor with wind surfing, volley ball and kayaking. Calm waters.
4. Euromanga – typical beach of the La Manga stretch, sandy and pleasant with calm waters.
5. Los Nietos – 4km long grey, sandy beach with showers, lots of restaurants and calm waters.

6. A group of 3 beaches – Cala Medina / Las Melvas / Levante – small beaches, with slightly wavey water, ranging from sand to gravel to rock, great all round beaches. There are restaurant services and some good opportunities for snorkeling.

7. Cala de las Mulas – a nudist beach with fine sands and no services.

8. Cala Cortina – a calm sandy beach with toilets and showers, and a life guard service.

9. El Portus – a quiet, sandy beach with showers, difficult to reach.

10. El Belonte Grande and Salitrona – a pair of short, sandy beaches only accessible by boat or on foot.

11. La Calera and San Ginés – gravel and sand beaches with calm water and reasonable facilities such as showers in places and a few restaurants and shops.

12. El Rihuete and Puerto de Mazarrón – sandy beaches, with plenty of local shops and restaurants.

13. El Cabezo de la Pelea and Las Covaticas – sand and gravel beaches which are great for snorkeling. Some of the coves in this area are frequented by nudist bathers.

14. Baño de las Mujeres and El Ciscar – this pair of quiet, short beaches offer great fishing as well as swimming and snorkeling.

15. Abejerro and Las Pulgas – sand and gravel beaches, quiet, with no facilities.

16. Punta del Fraile – only accessible by foot, with good clear water for snorkelling.

Take a look at Murcia Turismo web site (*www.murciaturistica.es*) for more details on every beach along the coast.

Part 2: Buying

This section will outline the process of buying in Spain, with particular tips on buying in the Murcia region. We highly recommend buying the following book, which was invaluable to us:

Buying a Home in Spain 2006 by David Hampshire
www.amazon.co.uk/exec/obidos/ASIN/190113069X/leanmarketing–21
ISBN: 190113069X, £11.95

This book is updated annually and covers the whole buying process in Spain, in detail.

Why Murcia?

House Prices

House prices have risen by 17.1% throughout the whole of Spain during the third quarter of 2004 according to figures published by the ministry for housing. This is an increase in the rate of inflation over the same period last year, which was 16.45%.

Prices rose most rapidly in Murcia – 25.39%.

Developments

There are 54 projected golf courses in the region, with 14 already built or being built.

A new airport is being built near Corvera which will increase the capacity for flights and ensure lower prices and offer greater flexibility to travelers. Whilst Corvera airport lingers in the planning stage, San Javier aiport is being expanded. The increased aiport service is also one of the reasons house prices are still increasing and more golf developments are planned.

The government plans to link Murcia up to the high speed national rail network, called AVE trains. This should be complete by 2010 to Murcia city, ensuring trips from Murcia to Madrid will be reduced from 4 hours to just 2.5 hours.

Murcia already has a great motorway network which is being extended with an east–west link bypassing Cartagena and linking through to Mazarrón and Águilas.

Greater water capacity is being provided through new desalination plants.

Retiring

After a life of working, what better way to enjoy your hard–earned rest than in a year–round, sunny, warm climate? There are health spas in places like Fortuna, Archena and the Mar Menor, providing specialised treatments. There are already many ex–pats here, so a thriving social life is assured.

Working

There is a growing tourism industry, with many tourist related job opportunites. Opportunities exist in the property trading business throughout the area. Many expats offer their services to one another using the housing estates as hubs for networking.

Murcia and Cartagena are well–developed business cities, with many opportunities for people who speak Spanish. There are some major employers in the area including GE Plastics.

Sport related work is available along the coast.

Internet access isn't a barrier to "home working" as ADSL has reached most towns in the area.

Buying Options

Going Native

There are parts of Murcia that have yet to be inundated with Brits, and these are the places where you will need to speak Spanish; your neighbours will be Spanish, the shops will be owned and run by Spanish people and most of your friends will only speak Spanish.

By selecting this option you will not only benefit from the wonderful climate of Murcia, but also from the rich and fantastic culture. If you're looking for a real change and challenge then this is the way to go. You must be prepared to work hard at integrating in your new community.

Countryside Properties

Renovations, fincas, village and town houses can all be found. In Murcia it's possible to find properties that are upto 20km away from the nearest civilisation. Often they will be up country tracks, with subsequent challenges in reaching them!

This brings its own benefits and challenges: fantastic views and peace, but the drawbacks include, fixing punctures on your car and the lack of some services like water, electricity and drainage, which you will have to make arrangements for yourself.

In Murcia you may well find that you need to take special care that these properties are not in protected areas. The best way to discover this is from an independent architect.

There are also properties within just a few kilmoteres of charming villages, where you get the best of all worlds, peace and quite, easy access to services and the village lifestyle.

Many Murcian villages have traditional single story houses, most of which were built about 100 years ago, with a central reception area and doors leading off to bedrooms, living rooms and kitchen. They are usually dimly lit, with small windows and thick walls for warmth in winter and coolness in summer.

Cities and Larger Towns

The majority of people living in Murcian cities and more modern towns live in apartments. This seems an aspirational lifstyle choice, though many people also aspire to owning a weekend hideaway in the countryside!

Choose your district with extreme care, spending some time in the locality to get to know it well will pay off in the long run, and help you avoid expensive mistakes.

Living in the city in summer can be noisy – you have to be happy to sleep with earplugs! The youngsters on mopeds, with helmets on elbows, and the late night revelrie can be exhausting. Of course you may wish to join in!

For those who crave daily access to their own stretch of beach there are some fantastic beachside towns with an authentic Spanish feel, such as Águilas. There are also a small number of houses near the protected coastlines, where new builds are prohibited.

Home Comfort

For those of you for whom learning a new language is daunting and you are really looking at Murcia's sunshine as it's principal benefit, there are plenty of opportunites.

From the coastal new–build housing estates and Campos de Golf, to the villages that have a high ex–pat population, home comforts can be found aplenty.

Within the newly–built housing estates you can find a range of properties from one bedroom apartments through to 4 bedroom detached houses, with as many bathrooms and a swimming pool too! Almost all of the new housing estates built for non–Spaniards have an en–suite golf course. In addition most estates have shops catering for all the Brit needs, including British staff and goods.

You'll also find bars and restaurants selling British beer by the pint, pie and chips and other such British gourmet fare! There are plenty of social clubs in Murcia, set up by and catering for Brits – from bridge to badminton; cricket to crochet!

Holiday Home

If you're looking for a property that you will only sporadically occupy, such as a holiday home then it's best to buy somewhere with higher regular occupancy. This will ensure people are around to watch over your home, and minimise your fear of bandits, raiding and looting (a popular concern in rural, remote areas).

For Investment & Rental

Just three words here – Location, Location, Location. Murcia really comes up trumps in this regard, with new regional developments (trains, planes, roads etc), superb weather, glorious countryside and unspoilt beaches.

Standard of Living

You'll save on eating out here. Our last three course evening meal for three people, with drinks beforehand, wine with the meal and coffees etc, totalled just €60. That's just fifteen pounds each! The daytime set menu can be as low as €7 per person.

COST OF LIVING COMPARISON...

	Britain	Murcia
Bottle of Red Wine	£5.00	£2.00
Pint of Lager	£2.50	£1.50
Packet of Cigarettes	£4.00	£1.00
3km Taxi Journey	£5.00	£3.00
3 Course Dinner for 2 (with wine)	£50.00	£30.00
Litre of Petrol	90p	60p

The region of Murcia covers an area of just over 11,000 sq km, with a population of a little over 1 million – that's just 110 people per sq km compared to the UK's 383.

Murcia has 18 hospitals, four international schools and three universities. Murcia University was founded more than 700 years ago, making it one of the oldest in Europe.

Looking

Never buy in Spain without first viewing the property.

Your Criteria

Make sure before you even start looking that you have an idea of what you want. What will you use your property for, how many rooms do you need, how much land, how often will you stay there, do you want to make money from your investment? Most often things go wrong when there aren't strong criteria for selection.

Draw up a wishlist, give this to your agents. This should mean that when you go to view they will only be showing you what you want and can afford, if they're not – stop viewing with them!

Viewing Checklist
(Make A Copy For Each Property You View.
Remember To Take Photos & GPS Coordinates)

Property

- ☐ Price _____
- ☐ Bedrooms _____
- ☐ Area (internal) _____
- ☐ Area (land) _____
- ☐ Gas?
- ☐ Electricity?
- ☐ Water?

Location

- ☐ Rural
- ☐ Coast
- ☐ Mountain
- ☐ Golf

Access

- ☐ Poor
- ☐ Fair
- ☐ Good

Notes (pros/cons etc):

NOTES
- Investment
- Rental
- Holidays
- For Family
- To Live

Additional Notes

Estate Agents

Estate agents in Murcia are little different from those in the UK, except that they should be treated with even less trust than those you left behind in Britain. The local Spanish press has run some amusing articles on how some of the estate agents operating in the region can totally misrepresent what's being sold, and put on a price tag that no local Spaniard in their right mind would consider. Estate agents take an even greater cut of the sale in Spain so will pursue a sales lead with rabid persistence. Therefore, bear in mind that local estate agents perceive British buyers as having more money than sense and there seems to be a never–ending supply of these walking cash dispensers.

All that aside, there *are* good estate agents, who are interested in your well being as well as their own. Just not too many of them! Make sure you check out the history of an estate agent, visit their offices and meet the staff – and most importantly ask for references.

You can look on the Internet and in the local expat press for their adverts for buying in the new Brit–oriented housing estates, and local papers such as La Verdad for buying in the cities.

Private Sales

If, and only if, you have a really good command of the Spanish language and have spent years in Spain, could you consider going 'off piste' and buying privately. However, never, never shake hands, pay anything or commit to anything before you have engaged the services of a local solicitor. The vendor will treat this with a great deal of suspicion since "that's not how they would do it" and "they aren't necessary and are a waste of money and time". You need to just play dumb at this stage and just say you need them to translate the paperwork for you and to understand the process, and the vendor should be a little more understanding. Usually the vendor will already be well–known to your future neighbours and probably related to them, so it pays to keep them sweet.

Developers

Just as property developers in the UK, property developers in Spain are on to a good thing. The first Hummer 4x4 we saw in Murcia was driven by a property developer, need we say more?

Our best tip here is that you will probably have the least grief if you buy a property that has already been built, either resale or from stock. Unfortunately there isn't a lot of that about in Murcia right now, especially in an expat–oriented housing estate. Therefore, you will be strongly persuaded to buy off–plan. Off–plan builds in Murcia have made some entertaining material for 'property nightmare abroad' TV programs in the UK. Those episodes probably weren't so entertaining for the unfortunate souls whose houses were featured – buyer beware. David Hampshire's book on buying property in Spain is absolutely essential reading for buying off–plan.

Purchasing a new property – New Build / Off Plan

If you have to pay the full purchase price before the property has been completed, by law, you must have the benefit of a bank guarantee to ensure that if the developer goes bankrupt before the completion of the building work, you do not lose your money. In some parts of Spain developers try to ignore this legal requirement.

You also need to make sure that the property specification is agreed in detail with the builder and that the property will be delivered to you complete with the necessary licence to occupy it as a home.

Fincas and Rural Properties

The building rules in Murcia change depending upon which municipality you happen to buy in. For example the rules in Fuente Álamo are different to Alhama de Murcia. Often an estate agent will have properties in multiple municipalities so you must take care to know what the rules for each are. Your estate agent may not know and assume blanket rules.

Before deciding to buy ensure that you will be able to rebuild by running your own check using your gestor, abogado and architect. Never trust the word of the Estate Agent.

In Whose Name Should You Purchase The Property?

In whose name should you purchase the property? In your name? In the joint names of you and your partner? In your children's names or in the name of somebody who will eventually inherit the property from you?

Each method has its own benefits and pitfalls, and it really depends on your personal circumstances, however, there are potential tax savings and other savings that can be made at a later stage. Tax savings can arise because of the Spanish system of inheritance tax as gifts on death attract high rates of taxation (sometimes well over 70% tax on inherited   wealth).

Each time a property changes hands certain taxes/fees become payable. If you can prevent the property being inherited and minimise the number of times it changes hands, you can greatly reduce your tax liabilities.

As with all tax savings schemes there is a danger that the Government can close the loopholes that allow the schemes to operate. In each individual case, you will have to weigh up the risks to ensure that your transaction is dealt with in the most efficient manner.

Get proper independent advice.

Pitfalls

As with estate agents the world over, their job is to sell you a house, and they're generally good at it. You must take care that you keep your criteria in mind at all times and not get carried away with the enthusiasm of the seller.

Private sales can suffer from confusion (sometimes intentional!) and family in–fighting. Always use an abogado and let them do the "negotiating"!

Buying from developers has a myriad of chances of it all going wrong, as you're only initially buying an idea! Read the small print, read David Hampshire's book, speak to other people, be wise!

A Brit's Scrapbook... Going Native In Murcia

Budget Calculator
(Make A Copy & Fill It In)

Property Price _____

Transfer Tax (at 7% on declared value) _____

Legal Document Tax (at 1% on declared value) _____

VAT – IVA (approx 7% on declared value) _____

Estate Agent's Fee (upto 25%) _____

Agent's Viewing fee _____

Travel (Flights/Car) _____

Notary Fee (approx €500) _____

Stamp Duty – New Properties (0.5% on declared value) _____

Deed Registration Fee (upto €500) _____

Maintenance Charges _____

TOTAL COST _____

For accurate costings see David Hampshire's Book ***Buying a Home in Spain 2006***. It's a complicated matter and there are many variables in the calculations.

The Purchase

Bank Account

A bank account is required for legal reasons and to access the large quantities of cash you will need to complete the transaction. It is very easy to do, select your bank, take your passports and NIEs and some Euros, it can be completed within minutes. Your bank cards and cheque book turn up some weeks later to your PO box (see below).

Charges in Spanish banks can be exorbitant and they are wide ranging. In Murcia, the Caja Rural is a popular choice for Brits, as their charges are incredibly low for transfers, and in some of the larger branches they have English speaking staff.

Money

You will need banker's drafts and wads of cash for most transactions during the buying process.

Cash machines frequently charge you even more than UK cash machines if you withdraw your cash from a competitor bank.

The People

Corredor

A corredor is usually a private individual working in the role as an estate agent. They will be taking a similar cut to estate agents. They are often gregarious characters, who can usually be contacted via the main bar in the town. There is almost always a family connection with any property they sell.

Abogado

These are Spanish solicitors – in Murcia it's usually possible to find one who speaks English. By comparison to UK solicitors you'll be pleasantly surprised by the reasonableness of their fees. They never usually expect cash up front, and will bill when the work is complete.

Their knowledge of the law may only extend to the rules in their region. There is huge variation in regional government in Murcia, so don't expect your solicitor to immediately understand all of the peculiarities, though do expect them to go away and find out!

Gestor

Basically a "gopher" – a licensed runner, who knows all the ins and outs of the paperwork and your local town hall. They can jump to the front of queues in ayuntamientos, while lesser mortals wait for hours. They are invaluable for lots of paperwork, not just purchasing the property.

Notario

A notary is mandatory in Spain and must be used when buying a property. They are equivalent to a local UK magistrate. Their main role in life is to stamp bits of paperwork to ensure the sale of the property can be completed.

The "Family"

Quite often, due to the inheritance rules, you will see many members of the family from whom you are buying, as they may all have to sign over the deeds.

The Paperwork

NIE – Número de Identificación de Estranjero – this document is for resident and non–resident foreigners, acting as both a social security number and an identity card. You will need this to open a bank account.

Escritura – these are the equivalent to the deeds to your property. It's a set of original documents which are signed and sealed by notaries, ayuntamiento and in some cases the seller and buyer. Usually you'll receive this document a few months after completion, after it has done the rounds at the ayuntamiento!

You should treat your Escritura carefully, place it in a safe place, in the bank for example.

Nota Simple – this is closer to the equivalent of the land registry document in the UK and is usually available for download by your abogado from the central Spanish registry, via the Internet.

It's good to always have copies of this after you've bought as you can use it to demonstrate your ownership of the property, for getting padrón (your electoral role), or buying a car.

Nota Simples are much easier to make photocopies of and are accepted as proof of ownership by most organisations.

Jenkins

Buying In Murcia – At–A–Glance

The following flowcharts give you an overview of the complete buying process from start to finish and can be used as your at–a–glance progress checklist and sanity checker.

- Step 1: In The UK – Planning and Research
- Step 2: In Murcia – Research Trip (1 week)
- Step 3: In The UK – Organise Inspection Trip
- Step 4: In Murcia – Inspection Trip (2 weeks)
- Step 5: In The UK – Get The Money
- Step 6: In Murcia – Finalise Purchase

DECIDE WHY YOU'RE BUYING

- ☐ Investment
- ☐ Rental
- ☐ Holidays
- ☐ For Family
- ☐ To Live

↓

DETERMINE BUDGET

- ☐ Mortgage/remortgage
- ☐ Staged financing
- ☐ Credit Cards
- ☐ Sell something/cash in stocks or options
- ☐ Get Financial Advice

↓

DO RESEARCH

- ☐ Read – David Hampshire book, this guidebook
- ☐ Internet – resources at end – look up estate agents, abogados, gestors, architects etc
- ☐ Decide which towns to shortlist. Use section 1 of this guidebook
- ☐ Recommendations – from friends, bulletin boards, magazines

↓

MAKE CRITERIA

Where? ☐town ☐village ☐seaside ☐mountains ☐countryside ☐urbanisation
Transport? ☐driving ☐trains ☐airports ☐motorways
Amenities? ☐hospitals ☐schools ☐colleges ☐nightlife ☐restaurants & bars
Type? ☐restoration ☐new build ☐off plan ☐pre–owned

↓

MAKE SPECIFICATION

Size? ☐bedrooms ☐bathrooms ☐garage
Outdoor space? ☐garden ☐patio ☐pool ☐trees

↓

ARRANGE RESEARCH TRIP

- ☐ Flights
- ☐ Accommodation
- ☐ Travel
- ☐ Meetings – Agent, Abogado, Gestor, Architect etc.

VISIT SHORT–LISTED TOWN/AREA

- ☐ Check amenities
- ☐ Visit Estate Agents
- ☐ Visit Developers / Collect details of properties
- ☐ Meet up with private vendors
  (people selling their own properties or Corredor)
- ☐ Meet Abogados, Gestors & Architects

repeat as necessary

CHECK IN POINT

Is this still what you want to do?
Is this still the right area?
Are your criteria correct?
Is your specification reasonable?
Is your budget adequate?

MONEY

- ☐ Ensure money is available & accessible (approx 15% of your budget)
- ☐ Select bank and make appointment to open account (need passport)

ARRANGE INSPECTION TRIP

- ☐ Flights
- ☐ Accommodation – hotel / B&B / Casa Rural
- ☐ Travel
- ☐ Meetings – Estate Agents / Vendors / Developers – send or tell them your criteria and ensure they have properties to match!
- ☐ Meetings – Abogados / Architects
- ☐ Meeting – Gestor to get an NIE
  (need passport & 2 photos)

VIEWINGS WITH ESTATE AGENTS/VENDORS/DEVELOPERS

- ☐ Be clear on criteria
- ☐ Be flexible
- ☐ Take camera and video camera – take lots of photos and video footage to help decide later
- ☐ Take GPS coordinates – especially for rural properties
- ☐ Make notes

↓

MAKE SHORT LIST

- ☐ Go to bar and compare each property against original criteria
- ☐ Deselect any obvious properties
- ☐ Have a big drink!
- ☐ Revisit properties alone – use the GPS coordinates!
- ☐ Meet with neighbours
- ☐ Check out local amenities
- ☐ Discuss with Abogado – is the paperwork correct, are they able to sell it, is it what & where you thought it was, does the nota simple look right?
- ☐ Discuss with Architect – can you do renovations, building works, is it architecturally sound, what are the likely costs involved?

↓

CHECK IN POINT

Is this still what you want to do?
Is this still the right area?
Are your criteria correct?
Is your specification reasonable?
Is your budget adequate?

↓

CHOOSE PROPERTY

- ☐ Make offer
- ☐ Sign contract
- ☐ Give deposit – usually 10%
- ☐ Set up bank account – Gestor can help
- ☐ Set up Post Office box for correspondence
- ☐ Organise NIE – Gestor can do this
- ☐ Select Abogado – choose an English–speaking solicitor and instruct them
- ☐ Have a bigger drink – you've just bought a property!

GET MONEY
- ☐ Make arrangements to acquire the necessary money
- ☐ Transfer money to bank account in Spain

WAIT
- ☐ Abogado will tell you when paperwork is ready

ARRANGE BUYING TRIP
- ☐ Flights
- ☐ Accommodation – hotel / B&B / Casa Rural
- ☐ Travel

COMPLETION
- ☐ Visit Abogado agent who will tell you plans
- ☐ Go to bank and order money – probably cheque and cash
- ☐ Go to bank and withdraw cash and get cheque
- ☐ Notario appointment (usually arranged by Abogado)
- ☐ Read through all documents in presence of Notario & sellers
- ☐ Hand over cheque
- ☐ Notario turns away – hand over cash portion
- ☐ Sign LOTS of documents
- ☐ Receive keys – congratulations, you've finalised your property purchase

RECEIVE DEEDS (ESCRITURA)
- ☐ 6–12 months after purchase

Jenkins

Part 3: Living

This section will look at living in the Murcia region. We highly recommend buying the following book for more general information on the whole of Spain, which was invaluable to us:

Living and Working in Spain by David Hampshire

www.amazon.co.uk/exec/obidos/ASIN/1901130746/leanmarketing–21
ISBN: 1901130746, £14.95

This book is updated annually and covers everything about living and working in Spain, in detail.

Whether you've bought a property or are currently renting, this next section tells you all you need to know about living in Murcia.

Moving

NIE – Número de Identificación de Estranjero – this document is for resident and non–resident foreigners, acting as both a social security number and an identity card. You will need this to open a bank account.

Taxes – Income tax rates are currently similar to those in the UK.

If you live in Spain (resident) and own more than one house, or don't live in Spain and own any house in Spain, then you need to pay tax on the 2% of the value of the house. This is because the government assumes you'll be renting it out.

Another tax that will be unfamiliar to Brits is the wealth tax (patrimonio). Which is levied on all of your property and possessions. Finally, there is a tax that is similar to the British Council Tax – called the IBI. This is used to pay for services in your locality.

Use a local accountant to make the arrangements and ensure you pay your taxes.

Padrón – this is the Spanish electoral role. As soon as you've bought a property or begin renting in Murcia, it is highly advisable to put yourself on the electoral role. This will enable you to have a say, and make your voice count in local elections. It has an added benefit of encouraging Telefonica to get your phone connected and enabling you to buy a car with Spanish plates.

Registering on the Padrón has no effect whatsoever on your tax status. The benefits are that the local council gets state aid depending on the number of people registered. This affects the number of local police, the infrastructure, waste disposal etc.

There are some areas where the actual population is 4 times the registered population and as a result the facilities are totally inadequate. Get down to the Ayuntamiento and register! It's free!

Residencia – Residents Permit – In general Brits who are employees or self–employed in the UK do not need a residencia. However, if you want to start a business you do need a residencia. The best advice is if you want to live in Spain for more than 6 months in the year then apply. For more details about the complicated rules, take a look at David Hampshire's book.

Pets

There are specific rules for importing different kinds of pets. In general, pets may be imported to Spain if they are accompanied by their owners or their representative and have a certificate of origin and health (if they are more than three months old). These are valid for ten days only, and must state that the pet has been under the owner's supervision for three months before being imported. They must also include a declaration that the pet is not intended for trade.

In the case of dogs, the certificate must show that the pet has had valid anti–rabies inoculation in the last twelve months (six in some cases). Certificates should be obtained from the nearest Animal Health Divisional Office in England. A full list of these offices is available by calling ☎08459 335 577, and at *www.defra.gov.uk*

Birds, monkeys and other species will need a certificate stating that there has been no local outbreak of disease that would affect the species for the last 60 days. For more advice please contact the nearest Spanish Consulate.

Owners who intend to take their pets back to England must comply with the Pet Travel Scheme (PETS), for their pet to be able to enter the UK without going into quarantine. For information on PETS, see: *www.defra.gov.uk/animalh/quarantine/index.htm.*

The tick and tapeworm certificate and the declaration of residence have been replaced by an EU pet passport. Only dogs, cats and ferrets (!) require a passport.

Culture

Murcia is a very sociable region, respect for elders and enthusiasm for children leads to a relaxed atmosphere, full of life and parties. Daily Murcianos can be found at their afternoon paseo or playing dominoes in the bar.

DAVID (THE ELDER)

David is our neighbour and all round good guy. He's in his 80s, regales us with stories of his adventures in France during Franco's time, shares his food and friendship freely and always provides us with massive entertainment.

His usual attire consists of motorbike slippers and a smart shirt. He is a bit of a property magnate, owning houses in the village, in the town and the huge cavehouse next door to ours. His experience and knowledge have been invaluable and his conspiratorial advice has kept us out of trouble on many occasions.

Learning The Language

You need to find a school with CEELE accreditation – Certificado de Calidad en la Enseñanza del Español como Lengua Extranjera. Bit of a mouthful!

CEELE is a Certificate of Quality in the Teaching of Spanish as a Second Language and is granted by the Spanish Department of University of Alcalá de Henares and the Association of Spanish Economic Resources.

CEELE – Central de Reservas
Calle Talamanca, 10, 28807 Alcalá de Henares (Madrid)
www.escuelai.com
☎ 918 831264

Abaco Centro de Enseñanza
Calle Cartagena, nº 2, bajo
Language Courses and Cultural Immersion Programs
www.abacomurcia.com
☎ 868 944460

In the centre of Murcia, this school allows you to attend to all levels of Spanish, modern facilities and a maximum of 6 students per class.

ABACO Instituto Hispánico de Murcia
Calle Enrique Villar, 13
www.ihdemu.com
☎ 689 00325
Spanish language courses at the Mediterranean Coast. 15 courses, different levels, special courses for teachers, wide range of activities and excursions. Accommodation in Spanish families or pensions.

Ferguson Group
Calle Los pasos, 2, Molina de Segura
www.fergusongroup.com
☎ 968 939063
Offering all types of English / Spanish tution.

Instituto Hispánico de Murcia / MasterSpain
Calle Enrique Villar, 13, Murcia
Spanish Language and Culture, Graduate, Professional Programs
Language Courses and Cultural Immersion Programs
Independent Private College
www.ihdemu.com or *www.masterspain.com*
☎ 968 900325

Oxford Academy
Calle Miguel Hernandez, San Pedro del Pinatar
http://maxpges.com/oxfordmarmenor
☎ 968 180297
Learn Spanish, exchange students for free. Study in the morning and do watersports in the afternoon.

Red Bus Camp
Apartado de Correos n°29, Lorca
www.red–bus.net
☎ 968 402949
Language camp for 12–16 year olds – lots of activities included such as sailing tennis etc. For 18years+ there's a new Spanish and watersports

(sailing, windsurfing, subaqua, and lots more) course based at El club Náutico de Águilas.

In addition, the majority of towns offer free Spanish lessons to foreigners who are keen to learn. The quality of lessons may vary, but it's worth checking them out. Go to your town hall for more information.

Entertainment

Radio

REM FM – 92.7 FM – has BBC worldservice news, lots of adverts and some well known, past their sell–by–date DJs from the UK. Useful when you first move out, as the adverts often signpost services that may be hard to find. Covers the whole of the Costas on different frequencies.

BBC World Service – only available on short wave at 198, 648, 1296, 6195, 9410 and 12095 kHz throughout the day.

Both of these stations are available via the Internet (if you're lucky enough to have a broadband connection) and satellite.

There are hundreds of national and regional Spanish radio stations.

Television

The only English language TV is available through satellite (see satellite section).

National Spanish TV is TVE1, La2, Antena3, TELE5, Canal+ (need a descrambler) – great for football and sport, lots of talking heads political programs, many cheesey soaps (just like in Britain!) and even the Simpsons, dubbed into Spanish.

Local TV – CanalSur, Canal9, Canal21, TVMurciana, TVEMurcia – lots of local talking heads, local news, local tourist programs which are very good and some rather dubious content in the small hours (take care with children in hotel rooms!)

BULL FIGHTING

Bull fighting is still a major interest in Spain. Many bars sport a bull's head as a trophy, surrounded by photos of famous toreadors. In fact in Murcia near the ayuntamiento there's a bull fighting club, with the colours and symbols of all the Toreros who've ever fought in the region.

DVD Rental

There are many DVD rental shops. In the rural towns the majority of films will be in Spanish, from which you may be able to select an English soundtrack. There are also specialist DVD rental shops in the housing estates where you can get a greater selection of English language DVDs.

Cinema

All of the films will be in Spanish, including the Hollywood blockbusters which will be dubbed. You'll pay around €5.50 to watch a film.

There are major cinemas in

- Murcia – Centrofama (multiscreen), Cinesa Atalayas (multiscreen) (www.cinesa.es), Florida Blanca, Multiplex Zig Zag (multiscreen) (www.cinentradas.com), Rex.
- Cartagena – Ábaco (multiscreen) (www.cinesabaco.com), Alfonso XIII, Teatro Circo.
- Lorca – Don Diego Cines (multiscreen).
- Águilas – Multicines El Hornillo (multiscreen) (www.entradas.com).
- Jumilla – Cine Color
- Los Alcázeres – Neocine Las Velas (multiscreen)
- San Javier – Neocine Dos Mares (multiscreen)
- Totana – Cinema Velasco

There are also two drive–in cinemas, Flipper on the road between Murcia and Fortuna (km 9) and Mar Menor in Santiago de la Ribera right next to San Javier airport.

Some housing estates show British films on certain nights of the week. Look in the local Brit newspapers and bars for showings.

TV & Satellite

In Murcia, the four standard BBC TV channels are available via the Astra 2D satellite (28.2deg East), for which you will need a *big* dish to get a decent 24h picture in the region. The good news is that at least you don't need any kind of subscription, you just need a bog standard DVB digital satellite receiver for about €150 – it's the 1.85m+ dish and its mount that will cost serious money (about €1000 installed) and you will also need somewhere to mount it!

If you want to get Sky in Murcia, you'll need that big dish, plus you will also need to blag a Sky subscription which is only available to UK residents with a UK billing and installation address.

An easier alternative might be to get BBC World from the Hot Bird 1 satellite (13 deg East) – this only needs a 90cm dish and no subscription card ('free to air'). If you find BBC World's content is a little dry, you can get BBC Prime with the same sized dish from the same place in the sky on the Hotbird 6 satellite. The snag is that your digital satellite receiver will need a Viaccess Conditional Access Module (CAM) which costs €50 and, here's the snag, you'll need to stump up €140 a year to the BBC plus a one–off €45 fee for the smart card itself. See www.bbcprime.com for more information.

Don't forget that you can also get many English–language radio stations via satellite too – and these don't require any subscription or smart card, just a basic digital satellite receiver. You really need a 2.4m dish if you want 24x7 decent reception of the home BBC channels, and even then, BBC2 can still occasionally disappear in the evening.

If you need more advice there are a number of web sites that are particularly useful:

www.satelliteforcaravans.co.uk, *www.lyngsat.com* and *www.bbcworld.com.*

Fiestas

Look in the Visiting section of this book for the dates of the main fiestas. Check your local bar for the calendar of dates.

On top of the local fiestas there are national holidays, which include Dia Del Año Nuevo, 1st January, Reyes Day on the 6th January, San José on 19th March, Easter in March/April, Trabajador on May 1st, Corpus Christi May/June, Santiago there is 25th July, Asunción 15th August, National Day on 12th October, Constitution Day on 6th December, Imaculada Concepción 8th December and Navidad on the 25th December

A BAD DAY FOR PIGS

November 11th is the traditional day to kill pigs for the winter and make sausages. You are only legally allowed to do this if you have a permit, but few people observe this "law".

Be prepared to take many days off for fiestas throughout the year. Shops close, people party, everyone gets merry. Don't strees about it. Hey, that's why you're here!

"INVITADO"

Once you are truly accepted in your little patch in Spain, there may be times when you go to the till to pay your tab and find someone has beaten you to it! This custom is known as "invitar", and you will find that the barman will say – you have been invitado, nodding towards the smiling benefactor at the other side of the room. Doing an invitado first can be a bit of a challenge and requires a game of stealth to be played for the rest of your lifetime in that neighbourhood.

Religion

Basically Spain is a staunchly Catholic country and Murcia is no exception – remember that Caravaca de la Cruz is one of the Vatican's five worldwide holy cities.

Cafés & Social Clubs

Many of the cities (Murcia, Cartagena, Lorca, Águilas, Caravaca de la Cruz, Archena, Mula etc) and larger seaside towns have cafés that produce a café culture, offering opportunities to pose on a Friday and Saturday night. In the more rural areas, there will be one or two bars that are the hubs of social activity, where you will see any family member from time to time, though mostly the men!

Kids

School

Spain, Murcia included, did not have a good track record of basic education, which was highlighted by an indpendent International assessment in 2002, showing that Spain was about 20th in a set of 31 countries that were assessed. Although Spain was ahead of Germany and Italy.

For basic education there are state funded and private funded schools.

Most villages and towns have their own schools providing there are enough children to justify opening. Otherwise there is a school bus to take them to the nearest school.

El Limonar International School
Calle Colonia Buenavista, El Palmar
Vocational Training, Primary or Secondary Education
www.ellimonarinternational.com
☎ 968 882818
El Limonar International School is a private fee–paying bilingual school founded in 1990 and governed by a permanent Board of Directors. The School is accredited by the Middle States Association and by the Spanish Ministry of Education. The student population is

comprised of over 15 nationalities including, English, German, Japanese, French, American and Russian.

Shoreless Lake School
Apdo. 239, Totana, Murcia
Secondary Education
www.slsonline.org
☎ 968 424386
Shoreless Lake School (SLS) at Murcia is the Spanish branch of SLS of New Jersey (USA), an American school established in 1991. SLS is a private, non–profit organisation accredited by the Middle States Association of Colleges and Schools (MSA); authorised by the Spanish Department of Education; all boys school for American, Spanish, and foreign students.

Big Kids

Colleges & Universities
Universidad De Murcia

Avda. Teniente Flomesta, nº 5
www.um.es
☎ 968 363000

Although its origins date back to the thirteenth century, the University of Murcia as we know it was founded in 1915, which makes it the tenth oldest university in Spain.

The majority of the University's facilities and buildings are spread over two campuses: the older is La Merced, situated in the town centre, and the larger is Espinardo, just 5 km to the north of Murcia. A third campus for Medical and Health Studies is currently being built next to the suburban area known as Ciudad Sanitaria Virgen de la Arrixaca, 5 km south of the city.

The variety of courses offered by the University of Murcia is organised into official degrees (diplomas, degrees, engineering and technical engineering), Undergraduate and Postgraduate degrees, independent degrees, academic specialisation and extracurricular teaching.

Universidad Politecnica De Cartagena
Plaza del Cronista Isidoro Valverde, Edificio "La Milagrosa"
30202 Cartagena
www.upct.es
☎ 968 325400

Cartagena universtity started out as a mining school in the late 19th century, but didn't gain status as a technical university until 1975.

The university retains a strong technical orientation focusing on engineering, agriculture and science. Cartagena has also built a good foundation of business studies teaching over the past 85 years.

More recently, Cartagena has added tourism to the portfolio of courses.

Conservatorio de Música "Narciso Yepes"
Abad de los Arcos, 2 –Apdo.98
Vocational School or Career College for Music
http://personal.redestb.es/angel.martin/index.htm
☎ 968 441514

ENAE Escuela de Negocios de Dirección y Administración de Empresas
Campus Universitario Espinardo, Espinardo
Business Administration – Vocational Training
www.enae.es
☎ 968 899899

Inforges
Calle Vicente Alenxandre, 13, Murcia
Information Technology, Multimedia, Computer Programming
Independent Private College
www.inforges.es
☎ 968 350011

Building Work

Here you'll find some specific Murcia notes about building work. For general information that is correct for the whole of Spain read:

Buying a Home in Spain 2006 by David Hampshire
ISBN: 190113069X, £11.95. This book is updated annually by Joanna Styles (*www.joannastyles.com*) and covers the whole buying process in Spain, in detail:
www.amazon.co.uk/exec/obidos/ASIN/190113069X/leanmarketing–21

Permissions

In Spain you need building permits for just about anything you do to the fabric of your house. This also includes lots of things that you might be considering doing in the garden. While in the UK you can build a patio, build low decorative and boundary walls, ponds and sheds as well as install or remove partition walls inside without planning permission, *technically* all of these things might need a building permit in Murcia.

Much of Murcia's inland area is covered by Natural Parks and protected zones (such as official forest areas). If you are fortunate enough to live out in *el campo*, think twice before approaching the Ayuntamiento for building permits. Even if you are out of a protected area, but not in an official urbanised area, you will probably need over 2.5 Ha (~ 7 acres) of land to start any major building work. In protected areas, this limit rises to 50Ha (over 100 acres!). Two things that you definitely want to avoid are: alerting the Ayuntamiento to something trivial and uncontentious beforehand and the other is forging ahead with major work only to be stopped half way through.

GOOD BUILDERS

We fortunately found the best builders, they came as a recommendation from David and have helped us in many ways. Their attitude to building work is that steel reinforced concrete is good and that everything should be bigger than you originally thought. They particularly like constructing underground car parks, and have debated with us on many occasions about our *need* for more underground parking.

On a weekend inspection trip, which we'd told the builders about, we were met in the village with, "Well if you'd told us you were coming we'd have done some work!"

We recently called the builders to ask them how work was progressing on the new house, they said "It's raining". We replied, "Yes, and how's work progressing?" – "It's raining – we don't work in the rain!"

Though their attitude has taken us a little while to understand and appreciate, the quality of their work is first class.

There are two classes of permit that are needed for building work in Spain, depending on the scale of the work involved and its potential impact on your neighbours. The larger works require that you have drawings professionally prepared and submitted along with full project costings including all labour (even if it's your own time!) and materials required. Smaller things (including most of the things that you would be allowed to do in the UK without planning permission) are covered by the term *'obra menor'*. The decision as to what category of work your job will fall into is ultimately the decision of the Technical Architect at the Ayuntamiento. If you are doing all the work yourself, the Technical Architect will use some rules of thumb as to the costings.

The building licence fee is a percentage of the quotation, and for *'obras menores'* this is often a very small percentage. For these smaller works, once you have the license fee established with the Ayuntamiento's Technical Architect, you will then be given a form to take to another department of the Ayuntamiento. Here you will be given another form to take to the bank and pay a few euros by way of a downpayment on the final fee. Once the bank has taken your money and stamped the form, you take it back to the Ayuntamiento.

Within a few months you will get your permit in the post and an invoice for the remainder of the fee.

MARCO POLO

I overheard a conversation between our builder Salva and the builder's merchant, Javier, discussing the name to put on
our bill. It went a little like this:

Javier – "What's his name?"

Salva – "Marco Polo."

Javier, angrily – "I don't believe you, what's his name"

Salva, in earnest – "No, really he's Marco Polo"

Javier – "You better not be lying!"

Salva, trying to hide a big, silly grin – "He really is Marco Polo!"

The factura (invoice) arrived, with Marco Polo, The Caves,
La Murta and Marcus is forever known as Marco Polo.

For larger projects you will need to submit much more information to the Technical Architect at the Ayuntamiento. You will need architect's drawings and costings (the *'proyecto'*) which must have been stamped by the College of Architects. A contract with Aparejador (Technical Architect), a copy of the Escritura showing ownership of the land and copies of NIE certificates.

The drawings have to be authorised by the college of architects (the authorising body), who will ensure that it all meets building regulations, before being stamped and returned to the architect. He will then hand it all over to you, and you must submit it to the Ayuntamiento with an application form. Most people have had to enter into a contract with an Aparejador (technical architect) who gets paid 30% of the architect's fee, for overseeing the build, which is a similar role to the old building inspector in the UK. They should check steelwork, drainage, structure, roof slab etc.

It can take upto 4 months to receive the licence. You must start work within 12 months, and are not allowed to stop work for more than 6 months otherwise the licence becomes invalid.

With a new build you really do need a licence and if the finished building is not as per drawings and licence details you may have difficulties getting the certificate of occupation. However, once signed off, most people feel at liberty to, for example, add permanent roofs to terrace beams etc.

If you're not sure whether to apply for a license then it might be best to talk to a few of the neighbours and get their opinions – they should know how things operate – or you could ask at local builder's merchants, or a friendly local solicitor/abogado.

CAVE LIVING

As you'll often hear, caves are warm in the winter and cool in the summer. Although Murcia isn't well known for its troglodyte inhabitants, you will sometimes see Cave Houses come up on the books of rural estate agents. Self respecting Spaniards tend to prefer properties of concrete and breeze block.

Alternatives

Wooden Houses

Wooden houses do require planning permission in Murcia. Installing a wooden house without permission will result in a fine, proportional to the size of the house and dependent upon its location. You may also receive a demolition order.

Interhouse – Poligono Industrial Lorqui
☎ 968 690035

Antonio Moreno – Murcia
☎ 629 628716

Caravans

There is no specific law, *yet*, in Murcia that prevents you from parking a caravan on any piece of land that you own. This is the loophole that many Brits have to use (once they've been sold a dodgy piece of land by a dishonest estate agent) in order to live there and remain within the law.

Terramueble – Cesigres
CasasMalu – near Fuente Álamo
www.casasmalu.com
☎   610 444432

DIY

For basic tools and materials, you should try your local hardware shop (ferretería). From these shops you should be able to get sand, cement, bricks, hand tools, basic plumbing fittings, some paints, floor and wall tiles, etc. We would encourage readers to use their local ferretería regularly since you'll regret it sorely if they go out of business!

For more 'weird stuff', like fibreglass septic tanks, water pumps for your downstairs deposit, a wider selection of bathroom taps, etc., you will be better off going to your nearest large trading estate (polígono). The best ones for electrical, building and plumbing supplies we have found are to the west of Murcia (San Ginés), to the north east of Cartagena and to the west of Lorquí.

You will find that suppliers on these trading estates usually have what you need ex–stock, at a good price and they often deliver a decent–sized order for free. Be aware that most of the trade counter outfits only accept cash, but this offers a good opportunity for substantial savings compared to the equivalent item ordered locally.

If you are looking for the warm feeling that UK DIY superstores offer, then you currently need to trek to the north side of Alicante to visit Leroy Merlin. This out–of–town shop has just about everything, but, as with UK DIY retail outfits, expect to pay over–the–odds for your individually shrink–wrapped widgets.

MAKING CONCRETE

For Marcus' birthday I bought him a lovely red concrete mixer! He was so proud. Our knowledge of concrete was limited, but it couldn't be that hard! We purchased the ingredients and got out our big book of DIY, and cheerfully began preparing the mixture. David, ever the helpful neighbour, decided to assist us. "Nice concrete mixer, you could do that by hand you know!"

We carefully measured the dry ingredients, throwing them into the rotating mixer, then began adding the prescribed volume of water. David, on tip–toes peered into the mixer and declared "Más agua!" (more water) – grabbing Marcus' arm and encouraging him vigorously. Marcus turned to consult the big book of DIY, and in a flash David grabbed the bucket and threw the lot in, "Más Agua!"

The mix continued to slosh as David skulked away!

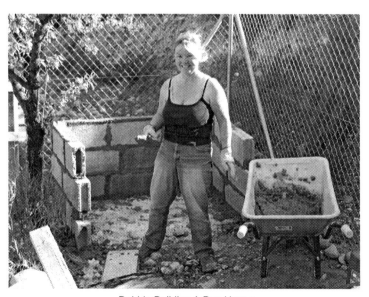

Debbie Building A Dog House

The Garden

Introduction

There are several good books on the market that cover gardening in Spain, and, together, you'll get most of the information you need to design and maintain your garden in Murcia. In particular, we found the following book excellent:

"Campo – A guide to the Spanish Countryside" – Sandy Walker – Santana Books – ISBN 84–89954–43–7
www.amazon.co.uk/exec/obidos/ASIN/8489954437/leanmarketing–21

There is one topic of particular interest to Murcian gardeners, however, that we didn't find covered very well in other books – how to make best use of your water! Read on…

Drip Irrigation

You probably know this already, but it's pretty sunny here in Spain, particularly in Murcia. For gardeners on anything but the smallest scale, that's a problem. You only need to glance into the newsagents here these days and the chances are that the headlines are about water, or more precisely, the lack of it. Farmers, in particular, are taking the brunt of the war for water (although somehow the property developers always seem to find a supply for that new golf course!). The desalination plants make water that costs them at least four times that which farmers in other regions have to pay. Drip irrigation is how all farmers around here make the best use of this most precious resource.

Drip irrigation can be useful for your garden and smallholding too! Since your water will be on the meter here, you too will be looking for ways to save it. Not only can drip irrigation save water, it can save you time and also keep your plants alive when you're away from home.

The first part of making a drip irrigation system is design. Plan a route for a 'main line' from the water tap and around the garden. This will be a semi–flexible black plastic pipe which has a 25mm (an inch) diameter. You can bury it under garden paths so you won't be tripping over it, but you'll want to run it on the surface near the plants themselves. The reason for running it on the surface is that you will be wanting to tap into it to add 'fingers' of smaller diameter, more flexible, tube that takes water to individual plants or groups of plants.

At each tree, or group of plants, you will attach a 'dripper' (or 'emitter' for the technical term) or a tiny sprayer (dripper for trees and large shrubs, spray for herbs, etc). Look at some of the Internet links on *www.lamurta.com/dripirrigation.html* for more details on planning the layout for different kinds of plants. Also, take a look around a Spanish farmer's field to see how they lay it out.

Special consideration needs to be taken if you are planning to feed the irrigation setup by gravity (from a water butt from your gutter downpipe or from a tank of irrigation water).

Firstly, since your water is not coming directly from a drinking water quality tap, a filter is even more important than ever. Secondly, you will need 'pressure compensating' emitters. These cunning widgets give out the same

---

WHAT *NOT* TO DO

Don't just get a hose and prick it with holes. Garden hose is expensive, frequently won't stand up to being left in the sun (unless you buy the *really* expensive hose) and the plants nearer the tap will get almost all the water and the ones at the end of the hose will get almost none.

Don't use "grey" water (from the bath, shower, sink, etc.). There are ways of using grey water for your garden, but drip irrigation isn't one of them. The drippers will clog up and the grey water will start to stink if it doesn't get out of the pipes straight away.

Don't use a sprinkler from a tap. This is the British way of watering; *so* much waste!

Don't get drip irrigation kits from DIY shops or garden centres. There will be a shop much nearer home that sells to farmers, will be much cheaper and you'll only buy the things you need.

---

amount of water, practically regardless of the pressure in the supply pipe. They are rated in terms of litres per hour (for example 4 l/h), usually embossed on the emitter itself. They really aren't much more expensive than other emitters, so it's probably worth using them in all installations anyway since they also get around other problems (like friction losses causing differences in pressure as the water moves from the beginning to the end of the system).

Finally, you will need some kind of head on the water, the more the better, so if you can make sure that there is at least a metre, preferably a couple of metres of head between the bottom of your tank and the first emitter, the system should work well. You can achieve this by putting the tank up on concrete blocks.

Now to shopping!

SPANISH GLOSSARY

Irrigation – *riego*
Drip Irrigation – *riego por goteo*
Dripper / Emitter – *goteo / emisor*
Pressure Compensating – *autocompensante*
PE – *politeleno*
Tank – *deposito*
Tube – *tubo/ tubería*
Hose – *mangera*
Filter – *filtre*
Elbow – *codo*
Tee – *te*
Coupler – *manguito*
Stop cock / gate valve – *llave de paso*
End stop – *tapón*
Big white cube thingys – *cubo de mil litros de segunda mano*
(para hacer un deposito de agua de riego)

You will need some tools, a saw (just about any saw, hacksaw, ripsaw, whatever) for cutting the tube, a pair of pliers for pushing the fittings into the tube, a pair of pipe grips for doing up the fittings on the thicker tube (unless you have hands like a gorilla) and, more specialised, hole punches for puncturing the tubes (different sizes depending on whether you are teeing off from the main line into the fingers or you are adding drippers to the finer tube itself).

As for materials, let's start from the tap and move on to the tree. You may need an adaptor for your tap to get on to the tubing. Then it's a good idea to add a timer–valve. These can cost a few bob to start off with, but once you have left the tap on overnight a few times, or come back from a trip away to find a scorched garden, you'll be glad you bought one. Next, you'll need a filter so your drippers don't clog up. Then you'll need the 25mm polyethylene (PE) pipe and at least one end–stop. You may also want some tees. You can buy the 25mm PE pipe by the metre; if the shop insists you buy a roll of 100m go elsewhere for your pipe. The same goes for the 12mm PE pipe you will need for the 'fingers'.

You will need some inserts (for want of a better word) that let you

---

INSTALLATION TIPS

<u>Install the pipes and fittings when it's warm and sunny</u>: The PE pipe is almost rigid when cold and very difficult to straighten out or to puncture for adding fittings.

<u>Pressure Reducer</u>: If you are running your system from mains water (a garden tap), you may need to install a pressure reducer just after the filter.

<u>Flush your system</u>: You don't want to have to re–install all those drippers if a handful of grit (or swarf from sawing the PE pipe) makes its way to the ends of the pipes. Lay out the pipes, make all the tees, install the filter but *don't* connect any drippers or install any end stops yet. Start the water supply to flush things through. *Then* install the emitters and end plugs (stop the water first!)

<u>If your system keeps blocking</u>: If, despite your filter, your drippers keep blocking, it's probably down to hard water. Farmers periodically flush their systems out with dilute hydrochloric or nitric acid. If you think this is a little dangerous for you, as well you might, you can install a reverse osmosis water softener at/before the garden tap – expensive but effective.

---

plug the 12mm pipe in as a 'T' to the 25mm pipe. At the ends of the 12mm pipe, you will need end stops (very simple affairs that you just stuff in the open end). You will need drippers / sprayers. Your design will dictate how many of which type. Finally you should buy a few 'goof plugs' (as the Americans call them) that you can use to plug holes that remain when you change your mind / garden layout (or, as their name implies, you goof and put a hole in the tube where there shouldn't be one!)

These materials are *cheap*; the 25mm tube is about €0.30 a metre, the 12mm tube is about €0.10 a metre, the drippers are about €0.25 each, 25mm tees around €1.50, 25mm end plugs about €1 each and about €0.05 for the 12mm end plugs. The only things that are 'pricey' are the timer valve (can be had for as much as €100, or as little as €20, so worth shopping around) and the filter – around €10. Go to another shop if they are asking much more than this.

If you are making a gravity–fed system you will need a water tank. We found that the white, metal–caged, thousand litre, metre–square plastic cubes (as seen all over the countryside!) that are second–hand containers from 'orrible things like hydraulic oil are perfect. You should pay about €50 each, plus delivery charges (handy if you have a trailer for your car, because the delivery can be expensive!).

WHERE TO SHOP

Your local ferretería or almacén:
Look for the term 'sistemas de riego por goteo' on their sign.

Miguel Muñoz in Fuente Álamo: A good price/English speaking trade–off.

Aldi/Lidl: For timer valves. Only for timer valves!

You will need to get rid of the remaining gunk that was shipped in the container (usually still has a label on the side so you know what you are dealing with). Then a good dose of washing up liquid, some coarse gravel, a few buckets of water and a helping hand to roll the cube around will clean out the insides.

You will need to cover the cube up, not just because they are unsightly, but UV rays from the summer sun will destroy the plastic when the cube isn't completely full of liquid. Black plastic sheeting (to stop the UV) covered by hessian (to look pretty) should do the job.

You will need to connect the cube's tap to your irrigation pipework – for this you will need a special fitting that comes from a drinking water container – your fereterría or almacén should know the problem well since the thread on the tap is 'weird' but it's a common problem. The special fitting usually needs some extra–thick PTFE tape or hessian and plumbers mait to stop it leaking. Don't complain – the special fittings only cost a Euro or so – if you want one that's made from turned aluminium, specially made for the job, they cost more like €25 each.

For links to useful websites take a look here:
www.lamurta.com/dripirrigation.html

General Stuff

This section includes stuff that didn't fit anywhere else!

Pets (*Mascotas*)

The general opinion is that Spanish people have less respect for dogs than Brits (have for dogs!). Whilst this may be true for "working" dogs (and you can always find lots of newspaper coverage in the English speaking press about cruelty to working animals) many Spanish people devote as much care and attention on thier beloved pets as we Brits do.

There are lots of kennels in Murcia that collect stray and abandoned animals. The most well known is Noah's ARC. You will find their most up to date contact details in any of the English press – or try this number 699 352 818. Noah's ARC is run by volunteers, with a distributed kennel structure. If you want to home (or foster) a stray or abandoned animal get in touch and make a donation. Be generous!

Cats can be found wild in almost all towns and villages, especially around Fish Restaurants!

You'll find at least one vet in every town. Many vets speak English and the standard of Spanish veterinarians is considered to be very high.

Fuggles and Dani Taking It Easy

THE LAW

All domestic pets in Spain must be identified by microchip or by a clearly readable tattoo. The tattoo will only be accepted as a means of identification until 3 July 2011.

Vaccination against rabies is compulsory. It is also advisable to have dogs vaccinated against other diseases such as distemper and hardpad. Cats should be immunised against feline gastro enteritis and typhus.

There is no law against dogs fouling public places, however people are becoming increasingly sensitive about it and there are specific rules within certain places, such as urban parks.

Dogs should be kept on a lead in public places.

The Spanish authorities have declared the following breeds or cross–breeds as potentially dangerous dogs when over 3 months of age:

- American Staffordshire Terrier
- Staffordshire Bull Terrier
- Mallorquin Bulldog (*Perro de Presa Mallorquín*)
- Fila Brasileiro (*Fila Brasileño*)
- Perro de Presa Canario / Canary Dog
- Bullmastiff
- American Pitbull Terrier
- Rottweiler
- Bull Terrier
- French Mastiff / Bordeaux Bulldog (*Dogo de Burdeos*)
- Japanese Tosa / Tosa Inu
- Argentinian Mastiff (*Dogo Argentino*)
- Doberman
- Neapolitan Mastiff

You must apply to the town hall (ayuntamiento) if you wish to keep or breed a potentially dangerous dog.

Stray dogs, if taken to the municpal refuge will be put down after 2 weeks if they are not claimed.

Pressure Cookers

Pressure cooking is a method of cooking in a sealed vessel that does not allow air or liquids to escape below a preset pressure. Because water's boiling point increases as the pressure increases, the pressure built up inside the cooker allows the liquid in the pot to rise to a temperature higher than 100 °C (212 °F) before boiling.

The higher temperature causes the food to cook faster. Cooking times can be reduced by a factor of three or four.

If you're old enough, you probably have memories of nasty, spitting pots, rattling around on the hob – dangerous beasts. These days pressure cookers are safe, efficient and your food will retain more of the vitamins and minerals.

The Spanish use pressure cookers more frequently than Brits, mainly because most people have bottled gas supplies for their cookers and hobs, and pressure cookers save lots of time and therefore gas.

You can buy a pressure cooker from any large supermarket and most ferreterías. We wouldn't be without ours now.

Google™ Earth

See, I told you this was the "stuff" section!

If you have a computer and Internet access, then download Google™ earth and take a look at your bit of Spain close up and personal: *http://earth.google.com*

No Smoking Law

Spain banned smoking in public places and work places in January 2006.

However, you'd be hard pressed to see much change in your small, local bar! This is mainly due to the badly written laws, which most bar owners are interpreting to favour smokers.

As of 2006, bars and restaurants that have a floor area of under a 100 square metres can choose whether to allow customers to smoke. Most have chosen to allow it, placing signs that proclaim Se Permite Fumar (It is permitted to smoke) on the door. Bars with a bigger floor area must have a specially set–aside smoking area. The overwhelming majority of small bars (and that means most bars in Spain) have elected to remain smoking areas. Spain's health minister has threatened that if enough bars and other small establishments don't elect to be smoke free within a year further restrictions on smoking will follow.

Native's Stories

Shh! Don't Tell Anyone…

Do you sometimes think that the Region of Murcia is Spain's best kept secret? Even the Spanish outside the region don't know about it! We discovered Murcia in 2001 when we drove down the La Manga Strip, it was love at first sight. The long golden beaches, palm tree lined roads and warm November sun, we were besotted and like the best love stories we let our head rule our heart and bought a property! We had not planned to buy a property in Spain, we were visiting the area to take photographs for our website.

We are not normally impulsive people, but we do have the motto 'don't just dream it, do it!' if we want to do something and we can afford it then we will do it. Our plan at that time was to buy a larger house in the UK, the mortgage was in place, we realised that we could buy an apartment overlooking the Med for the price of gaining another bedroom in the UK. Within four weeks we had paid the deposit and signed the purchase agreement.

The love affair with Murcia has continued and just keeps getting stronger. Since our first visit, we have visited the region every month and spent hours touring the area, as we sell property in the area it has been a case of mixing business with pleasure. We now specialise in selling property in the Region of Murcia as we feel it has everything to offer the holiday maker, investor and those wishing to relocate. We are also fascinated with the many undiscovered tourist attractions in the area and until this book was published, very little was written in English.

On our travels we have visited many wonderful restaurants, most of which look like a transport café from the out side, but turn into fabulous traditional Spanish restaurants with impeccably dressed waiters, linen table cloths and sumptuous menus. If you are really adventurous and don't speak Spanish you can always have the 'menu del dia' for 8€ (a three course meal with wine), we have discovered some wonderful dishes, especially the potato and meat stew which is served as a starter. We travel throughout the region and have already made a note of over 40 recommended restaurants, we are developing a tourism website, so that we can share these little gems with other adventurous diners.

The other delights that we have discovered are usually connected with food, such as the restaurant at the bottom of the cliff and over hanging the river at the Sanctuario de Esparanza, near Calasparra. Who would have expected to have found a church built into the rocks? The Spanish flock here in thee their hundreds on a Sunday, they also take picnics and Barbeques and meet up in huge family groups to exchange the news (rather noisily) There are so many exciting places, the Sierra Espuna with its fantastic views and you may see the wild boars if you are lucky, the bustling markets that are held in most towns, the wine regions of Jumilla and Bullas, the sacred cross at Caravacca and many more.

They also know how to party and can teach us Brits a thing or two. The magnificent costumes and traditional food and wine at their Fiestas which take place all through the year is another secret which we sometimes stumble on by accident, but once we have found them we make a note in our diary to return next year.

The love story continues and we are constantly finding out more and more, we feel as if we are still on honeymoon with years and years of getting to know the Region of Murcia ahead of us and hopefully there will still be some more surprises ahead!

Gill and John Hughes, Directors, Direct2Spain
www.direct2spain.co.uk, ☎ 0044 1743 364830

Bullfight in Cehegín

In 1974, whilst attending the Fería de Murcia, I stayed with my friend Gordon Morris at his new apartment in La Manga. We decided to go to a corrida in Cehegin on our way to the Fería de Albacete. I checked with the MIT Office in London and they said that there is a Hostal España in Cehegin, with Conference facilities and would I mind reporting back to them about it. Well, we set off from La Manga and drove through Albujón and Fuente Álamo (dusty and deserted) but before reaching Alhama de Murcia, we were stopped by the Guardía Civil dressed in full uniform (including 3 cornered hats). They wanted to see our international driving licences and passports (not like in the costas). I chatted in my poor Spanish and offered cigarettes. We laughed and were sent on our way. We were scared of these menacing police guards and I realise now that, as normal then, our hire car had a Madrid number plate.

At Alhama de Murcia we stopped for a soft drink (too much the night before) and Gordon pointed out a typical piece of Spanishness. A vine clinging to the terrace roof support was entwined by a yellow plastic rose. It is like the various oddities of Spain. How do you raise money to prevent cruelty to animals? You hold a charity bullfight, of course.

The road to Mula (which I notice is now marked green) soon changed from tarmac to grit. It was a long way to go, winding past a number of deep crevasses but we decided to continue. At Pliego the road improved as we carried on to Mula, Bullas and finally to Cehegín. No room at the inn, so, having secured our tickets for the corrida, we moved on to Caravaca, where we found a room, without baño, in the Hostal Victoria.

The bullfight started some 30 minutes late as the Aguacil, who had the keys, was nowhere to be found. He was drunk and fell off his horse right in the middle of the paseillo (parade). Qué escándalo! The dead bulls were hung in the main square where the townsfolk could buy the great chunks of meat being sliced off for them. In the bar of the Hostal España we were greeted with glasses of tinto. "You are not from here are you, you come from the city...Murcia?" "No" "No, ah yes from Madrid then?" "No" "Galicia, son rubios?" "No tampoco" "de dónde entonces?" "Inglaterra" "Oh...and how are the bulls there?" "We don't have them" "No...how sad, you don't have the fiesta? What a miserable country!" I somehow had to agree.

The next morning we set off for Albacete via Calasparra, never to forget our day in Cehegín.

Mike Penning

Our Dream...

My husband Ray and I had always wanted a holiday home in the sun. It was the usual dream of spending quality time with the family in our own small part of paradise, and swapping the long English winters for the temperate climate of the Mediterranean.

When thinking about location, we always came back to Spain for its weather and ease of access. Television programmes like 'A Place in the Sun' gave us an insight into the different areas of Spain, but nothing is better than experiencing for yourself the lifestyles and customs of the various regions.

No matter how we juggled the figures we just could not afford to have a home in England and Spain without compromising the quality of both. Reluctantly our dreams were put on the back boiler until our children had flown the nest and were settled with families of their own. During this time Ray had suffered a number of heart attacks and had undergone three lots of surgery. This resulted in him being made redundant from two careers! He had served 25 years with the Fire Brigade and 10 years at the BBC. The positive side to all this was that we now had a chance of fulfilling our dream of moving to Spain – lock, stock and barrel! We still could not afford to have homes in both countries, so it had to be a total commitment.

Surfing the web for more information, I was lucky enough to find the Direct2Spain website (*www.direct2spain.co.uk*). I rang the number given and spoke to Gill Hughes. We gelled at once and had a lively conversation about properties in Spain. I told her that our dream was to have a large piece of land with a finca – a typical idyll, but that we were open to suggestions. Other companies had refused to take us on an inspection visit until we were in a position to buy, but we wanted to make sure that we were doing the right thing before selling up in England. Gill suggested that we came to Spain with them so that they could show us their preferred area – Murcia, with out any obligation. She sounded so much fun that we agreed immediately.

We were not disappointed when we met Gill and John at the Murcia Airport, they were and still are, the nicest of people. They had arranged for us to see some resales in Lorca region on day two of our visit. Day one was put aside for exploring the area and talking through our requirements. I mentioned seeing a development on their website for new builds in Calasparra and although a new build was not really on our list of preferences, the style and size of plots attracted us. When we saw the show house, it was love at first sight (site!) Ray and I looked at each other and words were not necessary. We did not bother looking at any of the resales, we were hooked!

Reality set in when we returned home, putting our home on the market and borrowing against it for the deposit on the Spanish home. Although our family had been aware of our dreams and our constant talking about moving to Spain, I think it came as a bit of a shock for them to know that we were actually doing it.

During the next busy months we had some very bad news – Ray was diagnosed with mesothelioma, the asbestos cancer. We had by this time exchanged on the sale of our house in England and were planning to move to Spain and rent a property in the Mar Menor area until our house was ready. We were told that Ray had only six months to live, at the most, so we changed our plans and rented in England where he could be with his family and friends and with the doctors that he had come to know and trust. The next few months were very bleak and he died in February 2005. I was unable to make any decisions about Spain for some time. The prospect of moving on my own was daunting, but I felt I had to complete our dream, I know that time would give me the answer to the question of what I should do.

In July 2005 I decided to try to move to Spain and rented a flat on the Mar Menor. I packed my car to the hilt and got on the ferry to Bilbao. The drive through Spain seems a bit of a blur now, I felt so desperately lonely and sad. However I was lucky enough to meet some really nice people who lived in the same development permanently. They took me under their wings and showed me the ropes. After a few weeks I had settled in and felt that I might be able to stay and live in Spain on my own. I love the Spanish way of life and the weather is a huge bonus.

My lovely house is nearly finished and I am living next door with my new neighbours until I go to the notary in a couple of week's time. I am sitting on the front terrace typing this – the temperature is 26 degrees (today's date is the 28th March 2006) looking at the gentle hills that surround the development and down the valley to the town of Calasparra. There is a stillness, a sense of peace and a feeling that all's well.

Despite many obstacles, I am so glad that I have had the opportunity to fulfil our dream. At least I won't have to say 'if only…'

Dorothy

"Why Did You Come Back?"

My name is Mary I am 62 I moved over in 2004, with my husband who is 65, to a town near Denia. We moved into a typical Spanish townhouse with a lovely massive roof terrace, however, it was too hot to sit on in the midsummer, and icy in the winter. So that really was a waste of time!

But it looked nice.

In the summer the heat was unbearable inside or out you just dripped all day and felt sick for July and August. The winters were icy and the townhouses have a vent down from the roof, which makes them very draughty. When it rained, and oh yes it does rain, the street became a river with sewage floating along the cobbles and filling the deep drains and coming under doors.

Not what we expected at all, when we first moved it was hot and we wanted rain to cool us down, but we soon realised it was hell if it rained!

But the fiestas each month were amazing. It seems like the whole town dressed as Klu Klux Klan at Easter. The Moors and Christians are also something to see each July in most Spanish towns.

It was a nice town and the Spanish neighbours were lovely. But the doctors and some of the shopkeepers were quite abrupt.

The paperwork is unbelievable. No matter what papers you take to official places it is never enough and they change the requirements each week!

We expected heaven I suppose and it's not that.

We had always wanted to do it as we loved holidays in Spain, but living there is oh so different. There are only so many days to sunbathe on the beach before you get fed up.

People envy you but everything is harder to cope with and you miss your family. I have 10 grandkids and it was hell not seeing them very often. Cheap flights are hard to get hold of in the school holidays. But they came when they could. It was hard missing birthdays and special occasions with them.

I cried a lot then.

We returned because it was just not right for us, living abroad. We also wanted to be near to the family.

We think back on it now and miss the pavement cafes with lovely coffee, where you can sit all day and not be pestered to buy more, the sea at different times of the year. Many little things.

We also started worrying about being ill as we got older out there and did not want it to happen so far from home.

If you are an outgoing person and your family move too it's wonderful out there. But hard on your own.

Watching things like the little school kids being escorted by Spanish policemen as they walked along singing was amazing. Spaniards care so much for the children and put them first in everything

In Spain you go out for a walk and there will be a few teenagers in a band with trumpets just stopped on a street corner playing and laughing. They all respect their parents and you see them walking in the evening for a stroll with them.

To come back was not too bad as we found a little flat which is ideal to retire in. But I find myself missing Spain more than I ever thought. I was desperate to come back, but find England even more dirty and depressing than before we left. The news is always so sad, terrible things are happening and there doesn't seem to be any happy news

What advice do I have for others?

Think about it more before you decide.

Don't move for the sun it's hard doing shopping and stuff when it's hot. You are not on holiday; it is nothing like a holiday! If you do move take a duvet and hot water bottle and umbrella! Also take a kettle as they are hard to find. Keep sentimental stuff – don't throw it away. So much stuff I now wish I still had, but we parted with.

I am glad we tried it; we would have always wondered.

People ask us when they hear we lived there: "Why did you come back?" and we reply, "You try it!"

Mary (name changed)

Home Comforts

Home Sickness

No matter how well thought out your move to Murcia may have been, there may be times when you feel a touch of home sickness. You may miss your old friends or the speed at which your post arrives, the theatres and shows or the reliable electricity supply. You may even miss the cold drizzle on a Monday morning and the warmth of a good curry on a Friday night.

Home sickness feelings don't usually last for too long and often only strike when you're feeling low. Having a good strategy in place to ward them off and deal with them if they do strike will keep you from feeling blue.

Wisdom has it that there are three common stages of homesickness:

1. Exaltation – Everything is so new, fresh and exciting. You're living in what amounts to an entirely new world and every day is an adventure. This is kind of like the natural high that occurs to holidaymakers. It usually lasts for several weeks, or even several months in certain cases; but unlike the tourists, you're not going back home after soaking in a few days' worth of cultural sightseeing.

2. Frustration – Every high has to end sometime and usually it comes down with a bump. What am I doing here instead of going back home where I belong? I miss my friends and family. I miss wandering round my hometown and reading the local paper.

3. Acceptance – Well, things aren't perfect here, but things aren't perfect anywhere. By this stage you've learned to settle in and accept this society and your role here as it is. It begins to feel like home sometimes. You start to make a few friends among the locals, learn the language a bit and adapt to the customs and social norms.

Here are some ideas to help speed up the process:

Talk About It

Don't think you're the only person feeling sad. Your partner or neighbours may also get the blues occasionally too. Sharing your feelings will help, and you may be able to come up with ways to reduce them in the future.

Keep In Touch

Having a good connection with old friends and family enables you to keep informed about their lives and will also remind you of what you've got now. Keep in touch:

- Phone – make sure you get a good international cheap call supplier and call home as often as your friends and family can put up with you.
- Letters – the post in Spain is even slower than in Britain and can sometimes be quite erratic. Don't feel too heart broken if you think everyone has missed your birthday – the hundreds of cards may just be enroute or mislaid!
- Email – an infinitely more sensible and potentially more reliable solution to keeping in touch with friends and family. You also reduce the risk of becoming a pest as your loved ones can respond in their own time. This solution requires either a mobile phone device with email capability or Internet connection.

Keep in touch with other expats through online forums or social events. Here's a great forum if you want to "talk" to other expats:

http://brit.meetup.com

And some more online forums:

http://groups.yahoo.com/group/CostaCalidaExpats (quiet)

http://groups.yahoo.com/group/murciaexpats (quiet)

http://groups.yahoo.com/group/fincasinspain (never shut up!)

http://groups.yahoo.com/group/lifeinspain (can be good)

http://groups.yahoo.com/group/ExpatFocus

Think Positive

Make a list of all the reasons you came here in the first place – make the list long and elaborate, with all the reasons why you *left* the UK and all the reasons why you chose Murcia. Really make an effort with this –

include all your feelings and thoughts, no matter how mad they might seem to someone else.

Then the next time you're feeling down, review your list. Some friends of ours have scrapbooks with clippings and photos, to remind them of their reasons for leaving and why it's so great in Murcia – they add to them on a regular basis as new thoughts occur.

Get Involved in Your New Culture

One of the fastest and most long lasting ways to beat the homesickness blues is to make Murcia your home. Get involved in the culture, the day–to–day living, the fun and fiestas. Make friends in the ferretería and the fish shop. Gossip with the gas man and girls in the sausage shop.

It can be tempting to only mix with Brits, especially if you're living on a housing estate. This could be a mistake. Many Brits on the estates are only there sporadically, and seeing them go "home" may make you feel worse. Ensure you get a good grounding in the real Murcia.

Finally, if you're still feeling unhappy, then you may need to make the decision to return to the UK. Excellent resources can be found here:

http://britishexpats.com/forum/showthread.php?t=267933

www.direct.gov.uk/BritonsLivingAbroad/ReturningToTheUk

British Food

It's sacrilege I know, but now and then a bacon sarnie with tomato ketchup on fluffy, cheap, white Homepride is just what the doctor ordered. If you get sick of eating freshly prepared Spanish food, a quick drive to one of the larger supermarkets or the small specialist shops in the housing estates can give you your quick fix of fast British food.

And, if like us, you're missing something hot and spicey, take a look here: *www.ofistrade.com*

This company sources and imports ethnic food into Spain. Including Patak's curry sauces, which you can buy from: El Corte Ingles, Carnicas Campillo in San Javier, Upper 25 in Puerto Mazarron, Erosmer in San Javier. They also import Bovril, for those strange people who like it!

Resources

Newspapers, Magazines & Journals

In The UK

Living Spain
☎   00 44 01234 710992
www.livingspain.co.uk

A Place in the Sun
☎   00 44 01737 786 800
www.aplaceinthesunmag.co.uk

Living Abroad Magazine
☎   00 44 0131 226 7766
www.livingabroadmagazine.com

In Spain

Atlas Journal – Costa Blanca Monthly Magazine

Costa Blanca News
www.costablancanews.es

The CB Friday
www.thecbfriday.com
www.thinkspain.com

Costa Cálida Chronicle
Available in various shops in the area at the beginning of the month. There are also a couple of "English" shops in the area with noticeboards and social times. One is in Alhama de Murcia, called One Stop Shop next to the Centro de Salud (they have the Costa Cálida Chronicle at the beginning of each month, it goes quickly).

Another is in the Puerto de Mazarrón, called "A Taste of England".

Camposol, a new–build housing estate inland a bit from Mazarrón, has shops catering for Brits, they have noticeboards and publications too.

La Verdad
www.laverdad.es

La Opinion
www.laopiniondemurcia.es

The Reporter
Fortnightly on Fridays
www.reporternewspaper.com
☎   618 549283

The Informer
www.informernews.org

Vivir en el Campo
A really excellent magazine for those living in the country. Interesting/useful articles include reformation, cooking, nature, country travel guides, etc

It is different to other home/garden type magazines in that it has fewer adverts than most. Costs approx €3 and is published every two months: *www.vivircampo.com*

Expats
http://brit.meetup.com and
http://www.britishexpat.com/expatforum/country/viewforum.php?f=51

Newspaper Quotes

"Though popular with the Spaniards, these 'lost costas' [Costa Cálida] have remained mysterious to the overseas market until recently, as the coastal roads left much to be desired. Now that infrastructure has improved and the tourist industry is burgeoning, building is beginning but on a minimal scale. With strict regulations in many places, these costas are likely to be spared the concrete–jungle fate of the others."

The Independent
Katy Pownall
Published: 19 January 2005

"The Murcia region south–east Spain has much to offer including stunning countryside and beaches, fabulous golf courses, and, when the new international airport at Corvera opens in 2007, easier access to the UK and the rest of Europe. In fact, my wife and I are so impressed with the Murcia region that we are actually moving there ourselves.

"The Murcian interior is ideal for those in search of relaxation, nature and good food. The mountains here are full of wild game and lakes are stocked with fish. Quiet, sleepy towns, such as Calasparra, Moratalla, Mula, Bullas, Cehegín, Caravaca, Jumilla, Yecla, and numerous other localities are ideal for visitors and residents who want to lose themselves amongst pines, oaks and junipers, visit archaeological sites and experience traditional lifestyles. "

The Independent
Tony Sparkes
Published: 14 July 2004

"An emerging hotspot for property and golf is just south around Murcia, an underexploited region known as the Costa Cálida."

The Independent
Published: 23 June 2004

"Such a blend of flavours, a hint of everything that could possibly tickle the tourist palate. If ever a city could be called yummy, this is it. It comes in bite–sized pieces, too, a delicious little square here, a baroque confection there, a hint of hardcore Gothic over yonder, with just a dash of exotic Moorish flavours to add piquancy."

The Telegraph
Filed: 26 February 2005

"Yet without doubt, Murcia, on the south–east corner of Spain, is the next big thing to hit Spanish tourism and the international property market. Its undoubted appeal to the tourist and would–be property owner has gone largely unmarked. Until now.

This is good news all round, for local communities as well as foreign visitors – because it means that this astonishingly fertile, temperate and historic area has escaped the mistakes that have so marred other development areas in Spain."

The Telegraph
(Filed: 26 February 2005)

Recommended Reading

David Hampshire, Buying A Home in Spain 2006, Survival Books, ISBN 190113069X

David Hampshire, Living and Working in Spain 2006, Survival Books, ISBN 1901130746 4

Alec and Erna Fry, Finca: Renovating an Old Farmhouse in Spain, Santana Books, ISBN 84 89954 26 7

Sally Roy, The AA Map & Guide to Costa Blanca, AA, ISBN 0 7495 4335 3

Spain, Lonely Planet, ISBN 0 86442 474 4

Juan Pablo Avisón, Guía Viva Murcia, Anaya Touring Club, ISBN 8 48165 998 3

The Rough Guide to Spain, Rough Guides, ISBN 1 84353 261 1

Collins Bird Guide, Collins, ISBN 0 00 711332 3

Teresa Farino and Mike Lockwood, Travellers' Nature Guides Spain, Oxford University Press, ISBN 0 19 850435 7

For a bookshop in Spain with a good collection of english language titles, as well as games, visit your local Bookworld España store.
www.bookworldespana.com

Useful Links

A complete and up–to–date list of web links to estate agents, language learning resources, hotels, travel companies and other useful contacts for visitors and investors in Murcia can be found at *www.nativespain.com*

About The Authors

Marcus Jenkins is a consultant working for an international mapping company. He travelled extensively in his youth, giving him a taste for living abroad. Marcus took the fantastic photographs (*www.lamurta.com/?Photos*) chronicling the area, which are also available for purchase.

Debbie Jenkins is an entrepreneur, author, publisher and was a life–long city dweller who always longed for a place in the countryside. Her greatest excitement is in owning trees – hundreds of them!

Our Cave House is in the mountains near Corvera, 1 km away from a small village called La Murta, with a population (including us) of 101 people. The village is tidy and peaceful and inhabited by dedicated farmers.

In June 2001 we bought a small warehouse, attached to some caves, with 6.5 acres of land. We spent 4 years trying to work out how best to make use of our land, get enough money together to rebuild and renovate the caves and to build a wooden house as an interim solution.

In August 2005 we moved into our wooden house to enjoy the Murcian lifestyle – going native in Murcia – which we now enjoy with our two dogs, Dani and Fuggles.

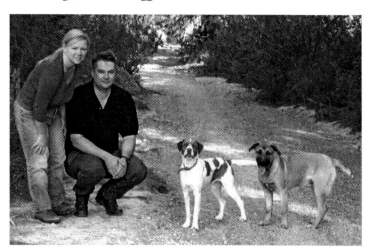

A Brit's Scrapbook… Going Native In Murcia

Our Story

Before we bought our place we spent about 2 years researching Spain in general, visiting the country about 8 times, starting in the Extremadura region in central Spain. This region had a lot going for it, especially the prices, which were around £20,000 for 5 acres and a house (2000).

We were unsure about property on the coast, being concerned about the bad reputation for too much development and too many Brits. However, we didn't want to let second hand information determine our decision so we "did" the south coast in May 2002.

Before we went out we did lots of research on the Internet, printing out reams of information. We spent 10 days on the south west coast and then headed south east to the Murcia region where we'd heard that prices were still very good and that it wasn't overdeveloped.

When we arrived in the region we were struck by how mountainous the landscape was; it was more like a lunarscape.

We'd decided upon 3 houses we wanted to view from one particular estate agent. The cave house was the first house we wanted to see and the last one the estate agent wanted to show us. They were far more interested in showing us pig farms in the barren valley – the house we wanted to see was up in the mountains. They showed us the house at about 5pm, on a very hot May day.

We knew straight away that we wanted it.

We'd seen about 50 houses by that stage, all along the coast, all in different states of (dis)repair. There were only 2 others that we liked. But as soon as we saw this house, we just looked at each other and tried to contain our excitement.

The location was perfect – it's just in the foothills of mountains taller than Snowdon, 20 minutes from the airport, with a new airport being built close by too (if all goes to plan!). And only 30 minutes from the nearest sea, the Mar Menor, Spain's inland lagoon. In fact we have approximately 250 miles of beach to choose from, the furthest drive being 1 hour.

We ditched the estate agent and then went back on our own and had another look. It seemed to us that the estate agents were quite deliberate in their attempts to confuse us about the exact locations of the properties, taking scenic and convoluted routes. We, however, were prepared. We had a GPS with us and had "located" every property, making a return, unaccompanied visit very easy.

Marcus can speak Spanish, so we returned when we thought the neighbours would be around. The property is one of 3 small houses, two of which are cave houses, set 1km outside a small village of 99 (101 counting us now) inhabitants. The neighbours don't actually live in their properties, they live in the village. These houses are for managing the land and fiestas.

We chatted to the neighbour David (in his 80's, he went to France when Franco was in power, and has strong views on "capitalistas"!) and he showed us the exact boundaries of the land – something the estate agent had been unable to do. As we walked around the land – all 6.5 acres of it – our love affair with it grew even more.

The next day we got all our credit cards, bank cards and what cash we had. Raided all the bank machines and got together the deposit of 20% – approx £4,000.

We made the offer and paid the deposit, signed a few documents and went back to England. That part took about ½ an hour.

Then in June we got a call to say all the paperwork was ready and they wanted the rest of the money!

This final phase took about 1 day in total, mostly waiting about in the abogada (solicitor) and notario (notary) offices. Finally a trip to the bank to pick up ½ the remaining fee in cash and a cheque for the rest – £8,000 in cash was a little worrying, as we had to walk through the largish town with it in a brown envelope.

Then the "deal" was done in the notary's office, with the whole of the Spanish family present. There was a lot of hugging and kissing – with the Mother (Josefa) who was the main vendor, and her 3 daughters and 2 sons, who all had to sign to agree to the sale.

The reason a percentage of the sale is conducted in cash is so that you pay less tax on the sale. Though it's not "legal" it's the usual thing. The notary turns his back when you hand over the envelope! But be aware, often around 4 years later you'll get a bill for the difference, along with interest for the intervening years. Don't worry, take it to your gestor and they'll get the amount reduced.

Here's what we bought for £20,000 – the estate agent's spiel, in full:

"Approx 20,000m2 land (permitted to build) part hillside part flat, planted with almonds, carob and olives, also large shed/warehouse with 3 caves at rear, mains electricity possible, set in the foothills of the Sierra de Carrascoy, nice views, 2km to small pretty village, 5km to town, access fair/good."

As it's a cave house, with a small house attached to the front of 3 caves, it's not the usual renovation project! We've had a number of builders and architects, all with different ideas of what we should do.

So that we could move out there sooner we decided to build a second property, which was (kind of) complete in August 2005, when we moved out there permanently. Our plan is to live in this second property while we manage the cave renovation project.

We identified some specialist cave builders in Granada (about 300 miles away), who we originally intended to employ from September 2005 onwards to renovate the caves, with the plan to move into the cave house in January 2006. Wishful thinking!

When we arrived in August 2005 we had no electricity, water nor an Internet connection. So most of our time has been spent managing (and paying) to get all that sorted! We quite quickly got the plumbing sorted (phew) and as I write this the poles for mains electricity are in the ground, not concreted in as yet, and standing at some wonderfully artistic angles. Up until now we've been using a mixture of petrol generators, car batteries and torches!

Running water we've solved by building a large deposit – a usual solution in the countryside (el campo) and buying various water cubes for irrigation of our newly planted trees.

Internet was a little more difficult as there is no phone link on our hill either! We got around this with the good will of David (and a few wireless internet tricks)!

The biggest challenge has always been the speed of getting things done. The joke about "mañana" is actually true. We're both very busy people and most of our spare time is still being spent chasing builders and sorting stuff out.

It isn't all plain sailing! We've had some ups and downs. Our dogs, Dani and Fuggles, have managed to collectively achieve: poisoning (twice), being shot (still has 20 pieces of lead shot in her!), getting hung in a wild boar trap, "fat face" three times (some sort of allergic reaction which makes his head swell up 3 times the size it should be and stops him from breathing!), and choking. All in the space of 8 months.

We joke that we should set up our salaries to go straight to our excellent (and fortunately very local!) vet. We know our way to his house, through winding lanes, in pitch dark, with dogs in various stages of distress, very well now.

We've also had an intruder.

We are fitting in wonderfully with our new neighbours – and they've taken to us as part of their extended family. Marcus has great Spanish and that's helping hugely. We're members of the teleclub – the only bar in the village, and traditionally used by the old men to chat away the day and have a little drink!

Josefa, the lady we bought the house from still lives in the village and invites us in for snacks whenever she can.

Frequently we find little packages of gifts, ranging from honey from the hives on the hill next door, to olives hand picked from the trees on the neighbour's land.

Before we moved here permanently we mainly flew from Birmingham with Mytravellite. Costs from Birmingham direct to Murcia average out at about £80 return. FlyBe also fly direct to Murcia from Birmingham. Our many visitors often fly to Alicante or Almeria – which takes about 1 hour extra driving time in Spain.

With Marcus' language skills we've managed to avoid lots of potential problems. We both went to the Brasshouse centre in Birmingham for lessons and we also have loads of tapes and CDs – the best are those by Michel Thomas.

There's so much we love about this region – above all though we love the Murcianos – the locals. They are so welcoming when we make the effort to speak Spanish to them and they've really made us feel welcome in our new home.

The city of Murcia itself is very attractive in the centre and a great place to relax. The protected coastline has some excellent beaches for summer, while the inland nature reserves in the mountains have an extensive system of trails for hiking and biking where you can walk for hours and not see another soul.

Before we moved over permanently, we needed to be sure we still had an income that didn't rely on our geographic location. Debbie's business was a mixture of Internet based publishing (www.bookshaker.com) and face–to–face marketing (www.leanmarketing.co.uk) with the odd professional speaking gig thrown in for good measure (www.debbiejenkins.com). Fortunately – by focusing on income from the publishing business (which is set up to work wherever she's based) and by having a business partner in the UK Debbie has only had to visit the UK once since we moved here.

Marcus' work was from a home office based in Birmingham with regular travel around Europe (Germany, France, Finland, Italy, etc.), so with good proximity to airports and a good Internet connection he's been able to keep his current job and just change his base.

As a visitor you have two choices: either do it the Spanish way or the "Brits abroad" way. For those favouring the latter option you'll find what you're looking for on the coast in Puerto Mazarrón and the golf complexes. You can order pie and chips with a pint of lager!

If, like us, you're more interested in doing it like a native, then a little effort with the phrase book pays dividends. Take your rental car to Lorca, Murcia or the Sierra Espuña and you will really be able to immerse yourself in the Spanish culture, even if you are only there for a week or two. You can quickly get to places where you'll only hear Spanish and enjoy what Spanish people enjoy.

Since moving we have a lot more variety in life and we're both much, much healthier. On a daily basis we walk the dogs in the morning and the evening and eat lots of local meat, fruit and vegetables.

We've had lots of friends and family visit us and the temptation has been to spend loads of time taking people around to show them what a great place Murcia is. But we still work full time so sometimes have to point them in the right direction. Which is another reason why we wrote this book! The book will help anyone who visits quickly acclimatise and make the most of the region.

Almond blossom at our home, in February

Index

NativeSpain™.com

Be in the next guide...

We're committed to ensuring the quality of our guides
and as such have set up a free membership site for
readers and natives to share their hot tips and updates...

In fact, we have ambitious plans to publish guides
like this for *every* region of Spain in 2008/2009
but we can only do it with your help.

Not only will you have free access to town guides and
native's diaries for every part of Spain, but you can also
contribute too. Perhaps you have a story to share, know a
great little restaurant or the best beaches in your area.

If you do then join FREE and get involved at

www.NativeSpain.com

Everyone who contributes at www.nativespain.com will get
full credit in the next edition of the Murcia guide and
exclusive "author discounts" on future guides.

We look forward to welcoming
you to our growing community!

**The Absolute Beginner's Guide
To Profitable Property Investing**

PROPERTY™
made simple

DOWNLOAD
FREE
PROPERTY
INVESTING
TOOLKIT!

This book will enable you to...

Add an additional, proven,
revenue stream to your business

Start building your nest-egg, in your
spare time, while still employed

Become seriously wealthy
working part-time hours

Invest positively in your future
and the future of your family

PETER STANLEY

www.bookshaker.com

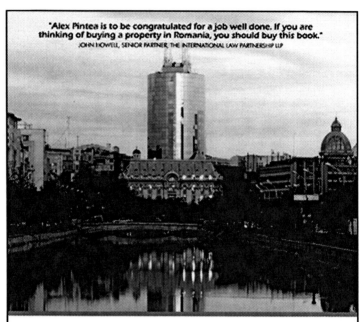

An Insider's Guide

Buying Property in
ROMANIA

The Essential Guide for Investors and Property Developers

Alex I. Pintea

www.bookshaker.com

ENTREPRENEUR

How To Create and Maintain Your Own
Portable Career Anywhere In The World

JO PARFITT

www.bookshaker.com

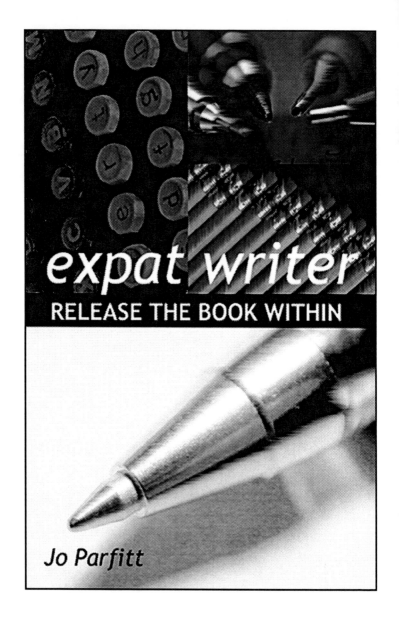

expat writer

RELEASE THE BOOK WITHIN

Jo Parfitt

www.bookshaker.com

Printed in the United Kingdom
by Lightning Source UK Ltd.
122445UK00001BA/73-78/A

9 781905 430215